Looking In for
Number One

Also by Alan Cohen

Books

Are You As Happy As Your Dog?
Dare to Be Yourself
A Deep Breath of Life
The Dragon Doesn't Live Here Anymore*
Handle With Prayer*
Happily Even After
Have You Hugged a Monster Today?
I Had It All the Time*
Joy Is My Compass
Lifestyles of the Rich in Spirit
My Father's Voice
The Peace That You Seek
Rising in Love
Setting the Seen
Wisdom of the Heart

Also available as audiobook

CD and Cassette Tapes

Deep Relaxation
Eden Morning
I Believe in You
Journey to the Center of the Heart *(also CD)*
Living From the Heart
Peace

Looking In for Number One

Adventures in Uncommon Sense

ALAN COHEN

Unity House

Unity Village, Missouri

First Edition 2002

Unity House is a publishing imprint of Unity School of Christianity. To receive a catalog of all Unity publications (books, cassettes, compact discs, and magazines) or to place an order, call the Customer Service Department: 816-969-2069 or 1-800-669-0282.

The Publisher wishes to acknowledge the editorial work of Raymond Teague and Michael Maday; the copy services of Marlene Barry, Linda Garrett, Mary Lou Kaltenbach, and Kay Thomure; the production help of Rozanne Devine and Jane Turner; and the marketing efforts of Janey Powell and Sharon Sartin.

Most quotations and factual material appear as they were originally published in Alan Cohen's syndicated columns.

Cover design by Cherie Peltier–Pimento Creative
Illustration by Margaret Chodus-Irvine
Interior design by Coleridge Design

Library of Congress Control Number: 2001099212

ISBN 0-87159-280-0

Canada BN 13252 9033 RT

Unity House feels a sacred trust to be a healing presence in the world. By printing with biodegradable soybean ink on recycled paper, we believe we are doing our part to be wise stewards of our Earth's resources.

*To Charles
and
Myrtle Fillmore*

For living in Spirit
and proving It is real

Acknowledgments

I am grateful to the editors and staff at Unity House, especially Michael Maday and Raymond Teague, for their invitation to share this material through Unity. My appreciation extends to all Unity churches, ministers, staff, and congregants, as well as the Association of Unity Churches, for their friendship, support, and teachings over many years. Truly ours is a connection of many blessings.

Special thanks to gifted singer/songwriter and good friend David Roth for inspiring the title of this book with his song of the same name and for giving permission to print the lyrics to "Looking In for Number One." David weaves marvelous stories and teaches rich wisdom through music, humor, and heart. To find out more about David's entertaining and uplifting CDs and concerts, contact him at <RothDM@aol.com> or <www.folkera.com/windriver/davidroth>. Also you may write or call him at P.O. Box 495, Orleans, MA 02653 or 508-255-9866.

In the office of Alan Cohen Publications, Michael Ebeling and Mary Traynor have been stellar shipmates, always showing up with grand vision, huge spirits, and the willingness and skills to serve. Thank you, friends, for lighting my life and this work.

I also thank my friends Dee Winn, Kimo O'Brien, Mary Beth Harnett, Steve Sisgold, and Bruce and Rachell Eckelman for their important comments and suggestions on the manuscript in process.

And thank you, dear reader, for opening your mind and heart.

Table of Contents

Introduction

One winter morning many years ago, I was awakened by a voice. It boomed: "Know who you are. You are not just a body. You are not just your emotions. You are not your experiences. You are a spiritual being, here to experience joy. God lives not outside you, but inside you, expressing through you, as you."

I sat up with a start. I was fully awake, and the voice was still speaking. This was not a voice within a dream or some random thought ruminating inside my head. It was a real person speaking to me from somewhere in my bedroom. I looked around, startled, yet saw no one. The voice went on:

"Your life operates according to divine order. Do not be fooled by appearances. Find the good wherever you look, and you can live the life your heart desires."

I leaned toward the side of my bed and looked at the clock radio on my night stand. The voice was coming from the radio. But speaking Truth? Who says intelligent things on the radio at 6:30 A.M.? I looked at the dial and realized what had happened. When I had gone to sleep the night before, I had been listening to a station I had just discov-

1

ered. Then I had set the alarm to automatic wake-up with the radio. I was hearing the station's morning programming.

And what programming it was! The voice, I learned, was that of Reverend Eric Butterworth, minister of a Unity church in New York City. I went on to listen to that voice every morning for many years to follow, and my life changed immensely as a result. I learned that the power I sought was within me; that God was not an old man with a long beard living on some distant cloud, but a presence of love in my own heart; that I was not subject to circumstances, and I could have a positive hand in my own destiny. As a result, I became involved with Unity churches as a student, and when my books were published I began to present seminars at them. My association with Unity and its principles has proved deeply rewarding and endearing.

Many times since that morning, divinely orchestrated synchronicity has shown up in my life, just when I needed it, delivering the message I most need to hear. In the Native American tradition, one of the wisdom characters is the coyote. Coyote energy is playful; it appears when you least expect it, keeps you on your toes, and always teaches you something profound. God is not just wise, but has a sense of humor too!

Years later, after several of my books had been published, I received a call from S. Virato, publisher of *New Frontier,* a popular New Thought inspirational magazine. Virato told me that one of his columnists was leaving and asked if I would like to take his place. Of course I would. So began a new path for me, one that has endured to this day and has expanded significantly. Now I write a monthly column, *"From the Heart,"* which is printed in many magazines throughout America and abroad. The material in this book is largely derived from my monthly articles. However, I have substantially edited and revised much of the original material, and three of the articles—"Honey, Do," "How Long It Took," and "Where the Answer Lives"— have not been published previously.

Looking In for Number One is a journey into your innate wisdom, strength, and wholeness. These real-life stories contain vital lessons that serve as stepping-stones for awakening. The message shines through many different characters: God is everywhere and love always works. Some of these tales will make you laugh, some will make you cry, and all will make you think. Over many years of sharing my intimate insights, I have come to learn that what touches me, touches you. As I discover the divine power that lives in me, you recognize the same in you. And so we grow together.

Here you will find fifty-two chapters to coincide with fifty-two weeks of the year. If you like, you can take one chapter a week and make it a theme for your week, a personal meditation. At the conclusion of each chapter, you will find three questions for personal reflection, which, if you answer them with sincerity and intention, will guide you to deeper self-understanding and spiritual empowerment. They will assist you to build practical skills to manifest greater prosperity in career and finance; love in your world of relationships; health in your body; peace in your emotions; and, most important, joy in your spirit.

You may also like to use the chapters and questions as a foundation for a study group. At your church, school, or with your circle of friends, you will find value in meeting

once a week to share your personal insights and to discuss what you've personally gleaned from the lesson. In such groups, the whole becomes greater than the sum of the parts, and your chemistry in joining together will take you beyond what you are learning as individuals.

Thank you for sharing in these adventures with me. As *A Course in Miracles* tells us, "When I am healed, I am not healed alone." May you fully manifest the life you envision, and may your journey be filled with blessings and miracles.

Looking In for Number One

I was looking all around
I was asking everyone I found
Do you know the meaning of
The mysteries of life and love

But I was getting nowhere fast
My overview was overcast
I picked up every book I could
I did the things I thought I should

I was looking out for Number One
Looking out for Number One
I thought that's how the world was run was
Looking out for Number One

But something didn't feel quite right
The more I looked, the less I liked
I networked, channeled, searched and such
I tried so hard to get in touch

And then one day out of the blue
My inner voice came calling through
"You have the answer in your heart
Try looking in, that's where you start"

Looking in for Number One
Looking in for Number One,
Looking out is not much fun
Try looking in for Number One

Looking In for Number One

I used to jump to my conclusions
Now I'm taking leaps of faith
Getting all my answers questioned
Looking in and seeing straight

Now I have the master plan
For finding out just who I am
It's not so much what others see
As how I look inside of me

Opening up to change and chances
Take retreats and make advances
Following your own Guru
Just spell it out, gee, you are you!

Looking in for Number One
Looking in for Number One,
Looking out is not much fun
Try looking in for Number One

I'm looking in, I've just begun
I'm looking in for Number One

Officer God

One Thanksgiving I hosted a gathering at my home. A friend baked a large turkey, but since most of my guests were vegetarians, most of the turkey was left over. The real beneficiary of the day turned out to be my dog Munchie, who was perhaps the most thankful of everyone there! I sliced up the turkey, packed it in little freezer bags, and gave Munchie a few pieces every day for a month.

When the supply of turkey finally ran out, Munchie refused to go back to eating his former diet of dry dog food. (Once you've tasted the big turkey, the little pellets just don't cut it anymore.) Then it dawned on me that I would have to get Munchie some more turkey. Being a vegetarian, however, I was not thrilled about walking into Safeway and buying a turkey.

Around this time, I was driving along a local highway one day when I noticed a police car behind me. Immediately I began to feel nervous (a genetic carryover from the '60s). Although I had not broken any laws, I did not like the idea of being followed by a cop. Suddenly I realized I must have been harboring some subconscious program about police, so I decided to reprogram it. I mentally affirmed: *The police are my friends; they love me and want*

to help me. That sure felt a lot better. I relaxed and let the fear go.

A few nights later, around Christmas, I was driving home when I encountered a police roadblock and I was pulled over. A policeman approached me and told me: "I am Officer K. of the Maui Police Department, and we are checking for drunk drivers. May I please see your license and documents?"

Sure, no problem. I gave the officer my papers; he looked them over and handed them back to me.

"Hey, Joe," he called out. "Come on over here."

Why does he need Joe? I wondered. And who *is* Joe, anyway?

Then Officer K. leaned back into my window, looked me in the eye, and asked me in a serious voice, "Would you like a turkey?"

"Excuse me?"

"We are giving away turkeys. Would you like one?"

"Is this some kind of joke?"

"No. You are not drunk, and your papers are in order. As a reward, we would like to give you a turkey."

Well, bless my giblets. As the old saying goes, never look a gift turkey in the mouth—especially when it comes from a police officer.

Before I could say, "Gobble, gobble," Lieutenant Joe was standing at my window, his hands outstretched with a huge, frozen Butterball turkey.

I must be on *Candid Camera,* I thought. Oh well, I can go along with this. I thanked the officers, hauled in the bird, and started to drive away.

"Wait a minute!" Lieutenant Joe called out. "We have to get your picture."

I am not making this up.

Officer K. got out his camera and tried to find the best position to take the photo. He kept stepping back until he almost fell into the stream of passing cars weaving in and out of lanes by drunk drivers. But the important thing is, he was getting a good picture for the *Maui News.* There I sat, under the floodlights of the Maui Police Holiday Roadblock on Route 31, posing with a dazed smile as Lieutenant Joe handed me, your model safe driver, and Munchie (in absentia), your model dog, a frozen Butterball turkey.

Finally, the officers sent me off, and I laughed nearly all the way home. When I arrived, Munchie met me at the door with his customary enthusiasm, barking joyfully, as if to share my holiday glee. I held the turkey up in front of Munchie and told him, "You are one heckuva manifester, mister. You got the cops to give you a turkey!" He just smiled.

This incident, unbelievable as it sounds, left me with a wealth of spiritual lessons. First, my affirmation to upgrade my relationship with the police worked. The moment I decided I didn't want to go through life getting nervous every time I saw a police car, something shifted within me. It's really not so different from Munchie refusing to go back to dry pellets after he tasted the turkey. Once you have tasted inner peace, living in fear just doesn't cut it anymore. There is only motion forward.

Second, my love for my dog (and his love for turkey)

set in motion a powerful intention to keep that big smile on his face. When you hold an intention born of true caring, life rushes to support you in amazing ways; when love starts to move, there is no stopping it.

Finally, the Universe took care of the details. My requests were answered almost immediately, without my having to struggle or strain to figure out how they could come about. I placed the order, and the production department did its part. Pizza Hut may deliver to your house, but when God delivers, you won't even have to get out of your car!

For Reflection

1. Describe a synchronistic experience in which the Universe manifested your inner intention in a miraculous or amazing way.

2. Do you still carry any old beliefs or programs that limit you? Choose one and formulate an affirmation to dissolve it.

3. Do you trust the Universe to take care of the details? Describe a situation in your life now in which you can practice trusting.

Maybe the Pharaoh
Chewed Juicy Fruit

*W*hile visiting Egypt, a member of our tour group found an unusual stone at the base of a sacred pyramid. The pink, round rock glowed with a mystical light, and as Gloria held it in her hand, she could feel a special energy about it. She wondered if it had been used by ancient priests for healing or perhaps even adorned the headdress of a pharaoh.

Immediately Gloria stole off to a private place and began to meditate, stone in hand. Psychically, she asked for images of the sacred ceremonies for which the stone may have once been used. After a few minutes, she was amazed to feel the stone getting softer. Visions of alchemy flooded her imagination; perhaps this stone was magic, a shape-shifter, transforming with prayer.

As Gloria continued to meditate, the stone became even softer, to the point of feeling gooey. Gloria could wait no longer; she looked down to see what the stone had become, only to find long pink strands stretching across her hand. The stone was a wad of chewing gum.

Our minds are powerful indeed, powerful enough to connect with God through a wad of chewing gum. What, then, is sacred, but that on which we choose to focalize our sacred thoughts? Everything is potentially sacred or

profane, depending on how we think about it. As Shake-speare declared, "Thinking makes it so."

True alchemy takes place in our minds. We transform lead into gold, devils into gods, and fear into triumph by employing vision that matches our intentions. A mystic can find God anywhere. As William Blake penned:

> To see a world in a grain of sand
> And a heaven in a wildflower
> Hold infinity in the palm of your hand
> And eternity in an hour

You and I might be in heaven right now and not even know it because we are paying attention to hell. We may be in the midst of great love, caring, and well-being. You may not be aware that God is in the person sitting next to you on the bus or the presidential candidate you didn't vote for or even the security guard who tickets cars at the airport. God is even in you just as you are.

The mind is capable of creating vast yet contradictory realities, all demonstrable in our experiences. A woman with multiple personalities was severely allergic to citrus in one personality (she would break out in profuse hives), yet utterly unaffected by citrus in another personality. A man had diabetes in one personality, requiring him to take insulin supplements; in another personality he was perfectly healthy; if he had taken insulin in that personality, it would have killed him. Perhaps this man is symbolic of all of us: we are healthy by nature, but via societal training, we have taken on belief systems that make us feel and act sick when we have lost touch with ourselves.

The game of life is won by finding beauty and good

wherever we go, no matter what appearances indicate or others' opinions dictate. Free will means that we may choose our thoughts and then live in the world our thinking has generated. God has decided to explore creation through billions of different vantage points (called you and me) for the fun of infinite self-discovery. One poet said, "God is a flower that grew a nose to smell Itself."

The story is told about a man who went to India to find a certain obscure saint. The fellow traveled over many rugged miles, putting together scattered bits and pieces of information. Finally, he found his way to a remote village where a shopkeeper told him that, indeed, the saint lived in that town, where he sat by a certain tree.

Eagerly the pilgrim rushed to the tree and found a man who fit the description. When he tried to converse with the man, however, the "saint" was disheveled and drunk. Put off by the erroneous information he had been given, the pilgrim returned to the shopkeeper and complained.

"Oh, that was the saint, all right," the shopkeeper insisted.

"But the man was drunk!" the pilgrim protested.

"Yes, he does drink a lot. But if you had stayed with him for a while, you would have heard great wisdom. You see, he is an enlightened soul who had but one more lesson to learn—compassion for those who drink. So he took on that experience to complete all his earthly experiences. Besides that one habit, he is an utter genius. If you could have seen beyond that trait, you would have found your saint."

And so it is with all of us. Everyone's garden has both flowers and weeds. We all have traits that others might condemn and qualities that speak of genius and redemp-

tion. Nothing is any one way, and everything is a matter of viewpoint. We make or break our lives with our thoughts. Meanwhile, God is in everything, and we find God if we look. If a sincere person in prayer can connect with an ancient mystical tradition through a wad of chewing gum, you and I can find our higher power through any avenue we choose.

For Reflection

1. Do you believe the Universe contains only one reality, or can you conceive of many different realities existing simultaneously?

2. Do you know anyone who in some ways has serious character flaws, yet in other ways is saintlike or a genius? What do you think is the Truth about this person?

3. Think of a characteristic about you that seems to be negative. How might you see this as positive?

Remember the Redhead

*A*tall man approached me at the conclusion of a seminar and told me, "A miracle occurred tonight." When I saw the tears in his eyes, I put down my briefcase and listened.

"A few weeks ago I felt very lonely, so I opened up the Personals section of the newspaper and searched for a girlfriend," he explained. "I called a half-dozen women who were seeking relationships, and I made a date with one. She suggested we meet on the following Sunday afternoon at a certain park bench at the city zoo.

"I arrived at the zoo a bit early, and my date was not there yet. On the bench where we were to meet, a redheaded woman sat waiting for her friends. I joined her and we began to chat. I liked her.

"Then my date came. We spent the afternoon together, and by the end of that time, it was clear to me that this was not going to develop into a relationship. Instead, I kept thinking about the redhead. She had captured my fancy.

"I went home and began to feel depressed. I wished that I had gotten the redhead's phone number; in contrast to my disappointing date, I had really enjoyed her. I began to beat myself emotionally. This has been the story of my

15

life: I always just miss out on good opportunities, and I wind up with what I don't want. I worked my way into a funk, and I felt horrible.

"Then I saw the advertisement for your seminar called *Looking In for Number One.* That phrase resonated deep within me; it reminded me that my purpose is not to find someone who will save me, but to find my own power inside myself. As I thought about reconnecting with myself, I let go of my upset about missing the redhead. I decided to simply take care of my heart and trust the Universe to help me with my relationships.

"Tonight I walked into the lecture hall, sat down, and looked across the room. And whom do you think I found sitting across from me? The redhead!"

Miracles happen when we give up seeking to be fulfilled by people and things in the outer world and relax into our own wholeness. Jesus advised, "Seek ye first the kingdom of God, and all . . . shall be added." This fellow's striking account of how he found himself *and* got what he wanted demonstrates that when we nourish ourselves spiritually, the Universe will assist us with our material needs.

I often ask people I meet, "What would you really love to be doing with your life?" I ask waitresses, taxi drivers, and passengers I sit next to on airplanes. Usually, people are startled to be asked such a personal question. Then they smile. No matter how frazzled, tired, or impatient they were before I asked them, they light up and become very present. If you ever want to see people transform before your eyes, ask them what is their dream.

I heard about a psychotherapist named Neils Logan.

Many patients paid Dr. Logan a considerable fee to undergo therapy with him, and he elicited gratifying results. There was a problem, however: Dr. Logan was bored. He had been a therapist for many years, and he was comfortable in his profession. But comfort is not always equal to passion. Dr. Logan's soul had shriveled, and he didn't even know it.

One day as Dr. Logan was listening to a patient talk about her life, he noticed he had been doodling. There, on the margins of his notepad, he had unconsciously drawn some rough sketches of sculptures he had been formulating in his mind. Sculpting, Dr. Logan had to admit, had become much more interesting to him than psychotherapy. When he became aware of where his passion truly lay, he quit his practice and devoted himself to sculpture. Now he is a renowned sculptor, commanding considerable amounts of money for his artistic talents.

Dr. Logan was sensitive to the signals of his soul, and he had the courage to move with them. Many people, however, do not hear their inner voice so clearly or act on it. In that case, life has an amazing way of moving us to our next adventure—whether we realize it at the time or not.

I met an attorney named Andrew who had lost his job through bankruptcy. Andrew confided in me that he did not really enjoy the practice of law, and it was no surprise that he went out of business. He was more interested in computers.

During his bankruptcy process, Andrew did a great deal of research on the laws of bankruptcy and recorded his notes on a computer. Over time, he collected a wealth of information and arranged it in a unique way. When he

realized that he had done something unprecedented, Andrew took his notes and program to executives at Apple Computers. They liked the program and offered him a handsome sum of money to flesh it out. Now Andrew is passionate and well-paid, working with Macintosh as a legal program development consultant.

The force of planetary and personal evolution is always moving, and it speaks through your passion. You can step toward your dream yourself, or life will move you. The key is to listen keenly to your instincts, accept your impeccable uniqueness, and stay on the cutting edge of your aliveness. And don't be fooled by appearances. The fulfillment of your heart's desires may be a lot closer than you think. Just remember the redhead.

For Reflection

1. Have you ever made a mistake that turned out to be a stepping-stone to success?

2. Is there anything you would rather be doing with your life? What would it take for you to actually do it?

3. Can you find wholeness and joy within yourself now, even before you achieve your goal?

I Can't Believe
It's Not Buddha

On the beautiful island of Kauai, I love to visit a magical stream that flows through a lush mountain valley. I usually enter the stream at a small eddy that forms a shallow pool. The first time I stepped into this pool, I noticed some accumulated natural debris on the bottom of the pool. Lovingly, I cleared away some sticks, leaves, and nutshells. When I thought I had restored the pool floor to a smooth surface of fine silt, I noticed a few more twigs and branches, which I tossed aside. Then a few more. As I reached below the surface and rummaged to get rid of all the debris, I discovered that the pool floor was *made* of debris. The layer of fine silt covering it was less than an inch thick; everything below it was rubble. If I cleared away all the debris, I would also clear away the pool's foundation.

The debris of our lives does not hamper us from being what we are—it *makes* us what we are. We tend to condemn ourselves and our lives for the difficulties we have experienced, when it is the difficulties that build our character. Dan McKinnon noted, "People are like tea bags—we don't know our real strength until we get into hot water."

Every situation is an opportunity to unveil the presence of love. Our purpose here is to find the light in as many different forms as possible. Our greatest calling, for

which we find the deepest reward, is to discover the divine in one another.

The story is told about a dying monastery operated by a half-dozen old monks who had become spiritually parched. One night a mysterious stranger arrived at the monastery. When the monks welcomed him, they recognized an unusual glow about him. The next morning they sat with their guest at breakfast, eager to hear his words of wisdom. "Last night I had a dream," he reported. "It was revealed to me that one of you is the messiah."

The monks were astonished and looked at one another, bewildered. "Who is it?" one of them asked boldly.

"That is something I cannot reveal to you," the stranger answered. "You will have to discover that for yourself." Then, as mysteriously as he had arrived, the man departed.

During the weeks and months that followed, the monks treaded lightly with one another and looked into each other's eyes more deeply. They treated one another as if any one of them could be the messiah. Then, over a period of time, something miraculous happened. For the first time in many years, joy and appreciation began to fill the halls of the monastery. A feeling of eager anticipation enlivened their prayers, meals, and conversations. As a result, people who visited the monastery felt uplifted, and the number of visitors increased. After a time the monastery came back to life, and the order was carried on by new monks who found refreshment for their souls.

Eventually all the original monks passed on, without any one of them being designated as the messiah. They all had become the messiah.

Wouldn't it be beautiful if we treated everyone as the Messiah, or the Buddha, or the Christ? Can you imagine the kind of world we would create? As Joan Osborne asked in song, "What if God was one of us?"

One day while I was staying at a remote retreat house on Maui, two fellows came to the door. One told me he had stayed at the house the previous week, and he wanted to show his friend the view. He introduced himself as John and his friend as Ken. I showed them in; they walked around for ten minutes, thanked me, and left.

Later that day I was walking along a nearby country road when an Aerostar van pulled over and the driver asked if I wanted a ride. "John Denver here, again," he greeted me. "Thanks for showing us around your house this morning."

I couldn't believe I hadn't recognized him earlier! I shook John's hand and told him how much his music had meant to me over many years. He smiled and we shared a moment of connection. A year later I learned that John was killed in a plane crash. Now I am so glad I realized who he was. That moment of meeting and thanking John was precious to me and means a great deal to me now.

In the midst of the debris or hubbub of daily life, we may discover jewels and great treasures. Never underestimate the potential of any encounter or experience. It may be God reaching out to you, saying, "Here is your moment of opportunity." In the "big picture," there is no true debris—just Spirit showing up in many forms to remind us how much love is available if we open up to receive it.

For Reflection

1. Is there any experience that you believe is outside of Spirit's plan for your good? Can you reframe such an experience so you see it as a gift?

2. Think of someone with whom you are having a hard time getting along. Sit quietly with yourself for a few minutes and find something you appreciate about this person. Keep looking past the debris until you find a friend.

3. Is there some great person you would like to meet and thank? Write this person a letter of appreciation, telling how your life is better because of him or her. If that person is living, send the letter. If not, keep it for yourself.

Healing Allowed

During a weeklong program I was presenting at a spiritual retreat center, several participants and I were eating lunch at a picnic bench next to a snack bar. As we finished, one of the participants stood behind me and began to gently massage my neck and shoulders. I, of course, was delighted to receive this kindly touch. I sat at the bench with my eyes closed, feeling my shoulder muscles unwind.

Suddenly I was jarred by a deep voice booming, "No healing allowed here!" I was certain this was another student playing a joke, and I opened my eyes to see who it was. To my surprise, the retreat center security guard was standing behind us. He looked the part: burly, a close-shorn crew cut, and a well-substantiated gut brimming over his belt. His name badge said "Gerald." I looked at Gerald in disbelief.

"I'm sorry," Gerald bellowed authoritatively. "No healing is allowed on the campus except in the healing temple. If you want to be healed, you have to go there."

I looked around at my friends and we cracked up. This had to be a practical joke. After all, who would make a rule against someone's being healed? I looked again at

Gerald and realized this was no joke. The student removed her hands from my shoulders and sat down.

After lunch I walked back to my room for a siesta. By that time I decided the situation was quite funny. And whom do you think I encountered along the way? You guessed it—Officer Gerald. I decided I would have some fun with Gerald. "Sorry about that healing back there," I told him. "I can't imagine what came over me."

Gerald remained quite serious. "I hope you understand. If I let you do healing there, before you know it, people will be healing all over the place!"

I had to muster all the will power I could to keep a straight face. I nodded my head and told Gerald, "And that's the last thing we would want to see happen, isn't it?"

"That's right," he answered firmly.

I dashed to my room, closed my door, and roared. This was too strange to be true. Then I remembered a Bible story that put my experience in perspective.

Jesus was admonished by the Pharisees for healing on the Sabbath. Now I'm sure that if you lived at that time and you were in pain and someone came along who could help you feel better—like Jesus Christ—you would jump at the opportunity. And if you knew someone who needed healing, you would love for that person to receive it, no matter what day of the week, right? But not the Pharisees; they had rules, you know. Later Jesus chastised them for paying more attention to the letter of the law than the spirit: "You strain at a gnat, and swallow a camel."

Now I'm sure Gerald was a very nice man, and he was just doing his job. But I took the experience as a lesson: I cannot afford to forget my deeper purpose because I have gotten caught in the details.

Yet there are less obvious ways we push healing away. We may believe certain actions are prerequisites for healing. Or we need to attain a certain level of spiritual purity before we can be healed. Or quit smoking. Or meet the right guru. Or overcome our sexual desires. Or be a vegetarian. Or have the right mate. Or earn enough money to have the right medical treatment. Or lose ten pounds. Or . . . or . . . or . . .

Healing can happen anywhere, in any way, under any circumstances, through any person or avenue. The Universe is always trying to deliver well-being to us. There are no obstacles outside of us. The only obstacles to healing are our own thoughts that run contrary to it, our judgments about who deserves it and how and when. No external condition whatsoever is required for healing. The only conditions are internal. What makes or breaks healing is our belief, our desire, our willingness, our openness, and our readiness. One thing is for sure: the moment you are ready and willing, the healing must come.

All that is required for healing is a little willingness. The real doctor is the mind of the patient. We choose doctors or external agents who tell us what we want to hear. If you want to be healed, you will find a doctor who will tell you that you can get better. If you hold some investment in staying ill, there are plenty of doctors who will substantiate your position.

When my mother was seeing an oncologist, one day I accompanied her to his office and asked him about my mother's prognosis. He told me it was not good. When I asked him if there was anything he could do for her, he answered, "We are not the masters of biology."

Right then and there I knew he and I did not have much to talk about. He believed that cells are in charge of the universe, and I believed souls are in charge of the Universe. End of conversation.

My mother, you see, was ready to leave. A few months later she passed away, but before she did, she told me that she was ready to go. She told me that she had had a good life, she was very proud of me, and she had done everything she had wanted to do. It was her choice to move on. Interesting, isn't it, that she chose a doctor who confirmed what she intended to do anyway?

There are many cancer patients who are not ready to go; they find Bernie Siegels, Deepak Chopras, Andrew Weils, and others who tell them: "You have a choice. If you choose to be alive and well, I can help you do that." These doctors would be the first to admit that they are not the source of healing; they are the agents chosen by the patients to assist them with their intentions—patients who realize that Spirit is the master of life, not biology.

Healing is allowed here. Healing is allowed anywhere it is chosen.

For Reflection

1. Is there anything you believe you need to do first before you can be healed? Are your prerequisites in the outer world or the inner world?

2. Do you believe in any dogmas that prescribe who deserves to be healed, and when, and how? Do you think God made up these rules, or did people formulate them?

3. Consider the statement that "the patient chooses a doctor who tells the patient what the patient wants to hear." Can you think of such examples in your own life or the lives of people around you?

The Miracle of
the Floating Fig

I arrived at Harbin Hot Springs at two o'clock in the morning, tired and hungry. I found my way to the locker room, peeled off my clothes, and immersed myself in the soothing, body-temperature mineral waters. Instantly I could feel my tired muscles, stiff and aching after a long day's travel, unwinding as they absorbed the warmth of the healing waters. I found a seat on the underwater ledge, leaned my head back against the rim of the pool, and naked before God, gazed into the vast starry night. Silently, I uttered a prayer of thanks for finding my way to this healing sanctuary.

But there was still a problem: I was famished. I had not eaten for many hours and, unable to find a store or restaurant during my late-night drive through the rural mountain region, I arrived without any provisions. The onsite restaurant would not be open until the morning. I began to feel anxious about not being able to get anything to eat until the next day.

Then I looked around me and realized I was in a place of great tranquility. An all-night candle radiated its mellow glow on a ledge just above my head, while a mountain stream chanted a playful lullaby just a few yards from the pool. Surely God was in this place. Though I was alone, I was not alone spiritually. Somehow, I reasoned, I would

28

be taken care of. Even if I had to go without food for a while, my heart was full.

Just then my reveries were interrupted by something touching my lip—an object had floated toward me and bumped into my mouth. I reached to remove it and discovered it was a fresh fig! Can you imagine my surprise and delight to find a sweet delicacy—actually, it found *me*— in the middle of a hungry night? In rhythm with the grace of the moment, I opened my mouth and received communion from a provident Universe—by far the most succulent fruit I have ever tasted!

Then I looked up to see I was sitting beneath a huge fig tree that spread its leafy limbs out over my entire section of the pool! Below the tree, I found many figs, freshly fallen, floating on the surface of the pool. I made a short round and gathered a handful. Then I went on to savor a most treasured midnight snack.

This experience has become a key metaphor for my life. It reminds me that wherever I am, God is. I am always taken care of, often in ways I could not control or plan on. The miracle fig arrived at the exact moment I surrendered my sense of need and remembered that all was well. What better formula for abundant living?

Now I recognize there are always figs (metaphorically speaking) wherever I go. *A Course in Miracles* asks us to remember, "I am content to be wherever He wishes, knowing He goes there with me." Perhaps Albert Einstein said it most eloquently: "There are only two ways to live your life: As if nothing is a miracle, or as if everything is a miracle."

My sense of awe continues to expand daily; I am recapturing the wonder of childhood, which faded from my life when I was taught that if I wanted something good to happen, I had to struggle to get it. Now I know that something good is always happening, and all I have to do is recognize it.

Not long after my fig encounter, I was waiting in the checkout line at a grocery store. In front of me a little boy, perhaps a year old, sat in the seat of his mother's shopping basket. I caught the child's eyes, and he burst into a huge smile. Then he began to giggle and wave his hands in ecstasy. This child was living in pure bliss. His joy did not depend on anything happening around him. Waves of delight were rolling up from inside of him and illuminating everyone around him. He was thrilled just to be alive and feel the presence of Spirit in him, through him, as him.

Jewish theologian Abraham Heschel wrote a classic book called *God in Search of Man.* We do not have to search for God; we just need to show up right where we are, and God will find us. My fig miracle was not an exception to the laws of life; it was the fulfillment of them. There are an infinite number of figs to be enjoyed and an infinite number of ways they can reach us. "Wherever I am, God is, and all is well."

For Reflection

1. Do you think that miracles occur through supernatural means or through the natural course of events? How might the Universe be using your daily experience as a means to deliver blessings to you?

2. Have you ever noticed that the more you fret and fight to make something happen, the more elusive it becomes? And when you let go, your request or something better shows up?

3. Are you wondering how a particular need right now will be met? What can you do to deepen your appreciation of the blessings here now?

A Public Proposal

*I*t was after 11 P.M., the overbooked flight was already an hour late for takeoff, and the crowd was getting grumpy. If ever there was a chance to practice peace in the presence of upset, this was it.

Finally, we were herded onto the plane and I settled into my seat with hopes of getting some shut-eye. As soon as we reached cruising altitude, the flight attendant's voice boomed over the P.A. system: "Ladies and gentlemen, one of our passengers would like to request your assistance with a special event he is planning when we land. Dave in seat 17B is going to propose to his girlfriend, who is meeting him at the gate. He would like you to help him deliver some flowers to her. If twenty-four of you would each get one rose from Dave and give it to his lady before he gets off the plane, you can participate in his proposal. Dave will show you a photo of Heidi . . . to make sure the right lady gets the flowers."

Ah, what a wonderful idea! I wanted to get in on the event, but I was seated too far from Dave to get to a rose before the other passengers. When we landed, however, I was one of the first off the plane, and I positioned myself off to the side to watch the romantic spectacle.

Sure enough, there stood a lovely young woman waiting for her man. One by one, passengers exited the aircraft, each with a red rose in hand. With a smile, each person delivered a flower to Heidi, who shyly received them. Then the passengers formed a semicircle behind Heidi, waiting for Dave and the Big Question.

Finally, all the passengers had left the aircraft—except for Dave. The flight crew exited, but the groom-to-be was still conspicuously absent. Then the pilot and copilot emerged. They closed the door behind them, commenting, "Well, I guess that's it for the night." The crowd stood silently, watching, waiting, and hoping. Had Dave chickened out?

Suddenly, with all the aplomb of a Hollywood epic, the airplane door swung open one last time, now to reveal a handsome young man in a bright sailor suit. Dave had arrived. The audience breathed a welcome sigh of relief.

The knight in white, carrying yet another dozen red roses, strode proudly to his lady-in-waiting (who by now looked like Miss America, flowers piled to her nose). Tears streamed down her cheeks as she nervously watched her man approach, knowing full well what was about to happen.

Dave presented her with the flowers and ceremoniously dropped to one knee. The audience was rapt. By now it was nearly 1 A.M., but no one was going anywhere. Over one hundred people fell silent and watched with awe.

Then he did it. He really did it. Dave produced a glittering gold ring and asked Heidi, "Will you marry me?" She tearfully nodded, and he slipped the ring onto her quivering fourth finger. With that, a great cheer and burst of applause went up from the jubilant crowd. The ovation reverberated through the silent airport, and probably still echoes today.

One by one, the group congratulated the couple and then we all made our way toward baggage claim together. The corridor was filled with laughter, chatter, and storytelling. People were happy.

Then something very profound occurred to me: the entire crowd had been transformed. Over a hundred people who had been tired, impatient, and frazzled two hours earlier were suddenly awake, joy-filled, and playful. Such is the transformative power of one sincere expression of love.

We have been told that our levels of energy and fatigue depend on the time of day, the number of hours of sleep we have had, stress, environment, age, and many other factors. Yet here was a group of people who had been awake for a long time, traveling under stressful conditions in an unnatural environment, and they had more energy when they got off the plane than when they began!

Energy and happiness have little to do with what is going on around you and a lot to do with what is going on inside you. You can find yourself in ideal conditions and be miserable, and you can be in the most adverse conditions and soar. Environment and physical factors may influence us, but attitude makes or breaks us. You may not be able to change your environment, but you can always change your mind.

Joy is the wild card of life; it supersedes every other formula for success. If you can find a way to generate joy, you can rise beyond all external factors. If you can play at whatever you are doing, you are the master of your life. And if you should ever have the occasion to make a public proposal, you can take a planeload of one hundred weary people and turn their evening into a party they will never forget.

For Reflection

1. Have you ever felt fatigued and then something wonderful happened that caused your energy to suddenly return? Was your fatigue physical or emotional?

2. Do you ever or often feel sick or tired? If so, what are you sick and tired of? Experiment with releasing yourself from debilitating situations (physically or mentally), and watch your energy return.

3. Have you ever done or seen a public expression of love that transformed everyone who observed it? What happened?

Your Holiness

When I read that the Dalai Lama was to speak at an upcoming conference, I noticed his name was preceded by the letters "H.H." I asked someone what those letters stood for, and I was told, "His Holiness." It's also the respectful title bestowed upon the Pope.

I began to wonder why the Dalai Lama and the Pope get to be His Holiness, but not the rest of us. To be sure, these spiritual leaders are very holy—but are they more holy than anyone else? Do the Dalai Lama and the Pope have any more God in them than the people who mop their floors? I imagine these renowned spiritual leaders would agree we are all equally holy in the eyes of God.

I met a man who called everyone he met "Buddha." "How are you doing today, Buddha?" he would ask me. "Beautiful sunset, don't you think, Buddha?" At first, I felt jarred by his magnanimous appellation. Then I began to really like it. It felt better than "Dude."

The story is told about people who came to Buddha and asked him, "Are you a god?"

"No," answered Buddha.

"Are you an angel?"

"No," Buddha replied.

"Then are you a saint?" they persisted.

"No."

"Then what are you?"

"I am awake," Buddha answered.

The goal of Buddhism, like any self-respecting spiritual path, is not to collect titles or make distinctions between degrees of holiness. The goal of Buddhism, along with mystical Christianity and other religions, is to wake up. I love the famous Buddhist admonition: "If you meet the Buddha on the road, kill him." This means that if you try to single out the Buddha and confine him to one form at the expense of all others, you have seriously missed the point. You must do away with your concept that this is the Buddha and all else is not.

A spiritual seeker named James heard about a holy man who lived in a house on top of a remote mountain. It was said that spending even a few minutes in the sage's presence could change a person's life forever. Hungry for awakening, James dropped everything and set out on a pilgrimage to find this enlightened being and look into his eyes. Over months he traversed mountains, valleys, and rivers to find the guru. Finally, he arrived at his front door.

The seeker was met by a servant who ushered James into the house and guided him through several rooms. Since he was so anxious to meet the guru, James hardly heard a word the servant was saying. After a few minutes the servant led James to another door, which opened to the backyard. The servant indicated to James that it was time to leave.

"But I was hoping to have even a few minutes with the holy man!" uttered James in frustration.

"You just did," answered the holy man as he closed the door.

You never know when the holy person you seek will show up, or in what form. The hierarchies we create ultimately distance us from God, rather than join us. The insecure mind takes refuge in pecking orders of spirituality, attempting to segment the universe into strata of power and worth. The Spirit of Love, on the other hand, will have none of the hierarchy game; all is God, all is powerful, all is spiritual, and all is worthy. As Sengstan, the third Zen Patriarch, declared: "The great way is not difficult for those who have no preferences. . . . Make the smallest distinction, however, and heaven and earth are set infinitely apart."

The "His Holiness" concept got me thinking about other appellations of respect. Take "Your Honor," the title attributed to judges. Certainly, judges merit honor, but are the other people in the courtroom less honorable? I suggest that judges address the criminals before them as "Your Honor" as well; perhaps this practice would bring forth the honor within the criminals. Most criminals were not treated with respect as children; doing so now might call forth their innate integrity. Socially aberrant acts are unskillful attempts to feel love, power, and attention. Addressing criminals as "Your Honor" might begin to satisfy that call in a healthful way.

Then there are "Your Majesty," "Your Grace," and "Your Highness" offered to royalty. Does that mean that everyone else is not majestic, graceful, or high? Hopefully not.

I've been thinking about what title I would like. I choose "Your Eminence." I like that because it implies that I emanate. That is my goal: to emanate. I want to emanate life, light, and joy. I don't care that much about being an Honor, Grace, Highness, or even Holiness; "Eminence" really makes my boat float.

So from now on, if you write, fax, e-mail, or talk to me, I respectfully request that you address me as "Your Eminence." And when it comes time for me to address you, I'll do the same. Either we all emanate together, or none at all.

Okay, Buddha?

For Reflection

1. Have you ever venerated a spiritual teacher with the attitude that he or she was closer to God than you were? How did you feel in this person's presence?

2. Have you ever met someone who thought you were closer to God than he or she was? How did this feel? What did you learn?

3. Have you ever met a holy, famous, or powerful person who treated you as an equal? How did this affect you?

Kissing and Driving

I saw a romantic greeting card that showed a couple kissing in the front seat of a car. The caption below the photo advised, "If you can kiss while driving safely, you are not giving the kiss the attention it deserves."

Anything that is worth doing is worth doing with a whole heart. And mind. And body.

We get into trouble not so much because we do things that are wrong, but because we approach our activities with divided intentions. Our bodies are doing one thing while our hearts are elsewhere. We go to jobs we'd rather not be at; we make love when we feel emotionally disconnected; we go to parties we find boring or repulsive. Meanwhile, we love people to whom we don't express our affection; we deny ourselves food we would enjoy; we stifle, deny, and delay our creative impulses; and we know truths we do not act on.

I have a very simple definition of *integrity:* You are in integrity when what you are doing on the outside matches who you are on the inside. I respect people who live unapologetically. I know people who do things I don't agree with or wouldn't do myself, but I respect them for being 100 percent who they are. They are in integrity.

In *Emmanuel's Book II: The Choice for Love,* Emmanuel

suggests: "When you move into your physical loving, as you remove your clothing, take off your mind as well. It simply is not equipped to hear the music."

In the movie *City Slickers*, a veteran cowboy named Curly teaches some angst-ridden nerds some country wisdom. When things get tough, Curly raises his index finger and nods. Eventually the city slickers figure out what he means: Do one thing at a time. If you can really focus on what is before you, everything falls into place.

I read a fascinating article in *USA Today* about *multitasking*, the process of doing several things at once. Years ago this was called *spinning plates*. Now it's *multitasking*. Whatever. The writer of the article posits that we invented time- and labor-saving devices to give us more time to enjoy life—but instead of enjoying life with our extra time, we find more things to do. Ultimately our lives are not richer because of our voice mails, e-mails, cell phones, faxes, pagers, Palm Pilots, and microwaves—they're just busier. If we used our extra time for activities that fed our souls, technology would find paramount service. But most of us just do more and feel less.

In the late 1950s, a survey asked a large group of people if they considered themselves happy. Nearly 60 percent of the group answered yes. A few years ago a similar study was conducted, and about 57 percent answered yes. So all of our slick technology has not improved the quality of our lives. Quantity of activities, for sure—quality, no. As Mahatma Gandhi pointed out, "There must be more to life than increasing its speed."

What is it, then, that makes our lives qualitatively better? Presence. Being 100 percent with what we are doing.

Approaching work, relationships—*everything*—with a whole heart.

I would like to tell you about the most prosperous man I know. Iani sits on a local beach and sings love songs. He plays exotic Indian instruments that he meticulously crafts at home. Each afternoon he comes to the beach around sunset and chants. He sings love songs to God, to the sea, to the sky, to the sand, to the wind, and if you walk by, Iani will sing a love song to you. During some very memorable sunsets, I have sat with Iani and sung with him. I take an empty, plastic water bottle and do percussion: low-tech, high-joy. Iani lives very modestly and has few possessions. He is the most prosperous man I know because his heart is full of love and he is fully present. When I am singing with Iani I don't miss my cell phone. E-mail is nonexistent. Money has no meaning. I am content.

"But not all of us have the luxury of sitting and chanting on a Maui beach," you say. "Some of us have jobs and families to support and responsibilities."

Yes, that's true. But presence doesn't require specific conditions. Ecstatic poets like Rumi, Hafiz, and Walt Whitman found and celebrated God wherever they went, in all things, with all people. Just be total. Bring all of yourself to whatever you are doing. When you are at work, that's all that exists. When you are making love, make total love. When you are with your kids, really be with your kids. One.

I noticed that when I did book signings, I felt rushed because I wanted to accommodate everyone in line. I was not fully present with some people because I was aware of the people behind them in line. Then I realized I was cheating them and myself. So I decided to be fully present with each person and stay with him or her until we really connected. Suddenly book signings became a delight. Now I love talking to people, touching them, looking into their eyes. I learned that it does not take a lot of time to make contact: just a few moments of full presence can be completely fulfilling.

Everything is like kissing and driving. If you're driving, really drive. If you're kissing, really kiss.

For Reflection

1. Remember a time when you were deeply immersed in a moment. How did it feel? What was your perspective on life?

2. Do you rush through some activities in a mechanical way? How do you feel while you are doing them, and afterward?

3. Choose an activity to which you would like to bring more presence. How could you do it differently so it would be more rewarding? Imagine doing this with a whole heart, and notice how you feel.

From "Should" to "Would"

My young neighbor Matthew keeps me on my toes. Matthew asks a lot of questions that I am sometimes tempted to dismiss as childish. But when I think about them, I find he has some pretty enlightening things to say. Quite often Matthew leaves me with a profound lesson.

One day Matthew asked me for a ride to the local grocery store so he could buy some popcorn. (He would live on popcorn if his mother let him.) I told Matthew I could drive him to the store, but since I was going on into town, he would have to walk home, a hike he often takes.

Then Matthew asked me: "What do you think, Alan? Should I go with you?"

"Whatever you like, Matthew," I answered. "It's up to you."

"But what do you think I should do?" he asked again.

I thought about it for a moment, and I realized there was no "should" about it. My opinion of what he should do was irrelevant. His decision depended entirely on what he felt like doing.

"Do whatever you would like," I told him. "If you want to go, I'll be happy to drive you. If you don't feel like going, you can stay home and play video games or whatever you like. It's up to you."

This dialogue went on for a few more rounds, until I told Matthew I was ready to leave. Suddenly he announced, "Okay, I'll go!" and he jumped into the car with me.

After I dropped off Matthew, I realized he was mirroring a part of myself that tries to find out what I should do when there is no "should" about it—only a "would." Sometimes when I am faced with a decision, I try to figure out how the various options fit into God's plan for my destiny. But God's plan for my destiny is happiness; if something would truly make me happy, behold God's plan for my destiny. Instead of asking some remote God who lives on a distant cloud what I should do, I simply need to ask the God within me what to do. God's frequency is pure joy. What I should do is what I *would* do.

The world is full of "shoulds" dictated by external sources. Religion, society, family, industry, and peers have all kinds of ideas about who you should be and what you should do. But no one outside you can know your personal path as well as you. Some of their "shoulds" match your "woulds," and many don't. Many people fall back on the apparent security of paths prescribed by external voices. Yet a smaller number of independent souls, probably such as you, find aliveness more attractive than convention. *Convention* means "convenient." It is convenient to take the well-trod route, for no one questions or challenges you. Yet those who take orders from outside sources do so at the dear cost of their full aliveness—a terrible trade-off, to be sure.

The highest morality is personal integrity. You are in integrity when your external acts match your inner knowing. When you forsake your truth to please others, you fall out of integrity. Robert Louis Stevenson boldly declared, "To know what you prefer instead of humbly saying 'Amen' to what the world tells that you ought to prefer, is to have kept your soul alive." And nothing is more important than keeping your soul alive.

In the film *Tin Cup*, Kevin Costner's character proclaims, "When the defining moment comes along, you define the moment or the moment defines you." We have been led to believe that life determines who we are, when at every moment we determine what our life is. Your decisions are honorable because they are your own.

One strong metaphor for attuning to your guidance is the cell phone. I hear cell phones ring nearly everywhere I go in public. Sometimes when I stand in line at an airport, I hear several people within arm's reach chatting away on their cell phones. I find it interesting that each person's cell phone has a distinctive ring. If everyone's phone had the same ring, no one in a crowd would know who was being called.

Your soul's calling also has a distinct tone. But you have to know its frequency before you can answer it. The more you live by external "shoulds," the farther you drift from the great love affair with your own spirit. The more you trust in your soul's calling and hearken unto it, the more you live in profound love. As a Chasidic sage nobly stated, "Everyone should carefully observe which way his heart draws him, and then choose that way with all his strength."

For Reflection

1. Is there some question or decision you are struggling with, wondering what you should do? For a moment, put aside your quest for "should" and ask yourself, "What would I do?"

2. To what people, groups, or institutions have you looked to dictate your "shoulds"? What usually happens when you follow an external dictum? Contrast this experience with the feelings and results you get when you follow your internal guidance.

3. Remember one defining moment in your life. Why was it defining, and what was your role in how your life changed as a result of it?

Magnetic Innocence

One evening I attended a screening of several video clips of paranormal and supernatural phenomena. One of the more humorous segments depicted "The Magnetic Family" of the Philippines—a family whose bodies, for some unknown reason, are magnetized to such a high degree that metal objects hold fast to their skin. The audience gasped and laughed to see paper clips, metal forks, and even a steam iron stuck to the bodies of this family, sheerly by magnetic force.

After the presentation, the organizer introduced me to the group, and for a joke, I called myself "The Magnetic Man of Maui." As I was standing on a porch outside the screening room, a seven-year-old girl approached me and tugged on my hand. I looked down to recognize her as one of several children at the screening. Without a word, the girl took a quarter from her hand and pressed it to my bare forearm. At first, I thought she was trying to give me the quarter, but then when the quarter fell to the ground, she frowned, looked up, and exclaimed, "I thought you said you were magnetic!"

I laughed, but then I realized the child was serious. Then I had a striking realization: *An innocent mind is open to all possibilities*. Jesus taught that if you want to live in a heavenly consciousness, you must become like a little child. Children abide in a magical universe. So do we, but we have been taught to question everything. Questioning is healthful, but not if it robs us of joy. Children believe things until proven otherwise; perhaps we would do well to trust more and doubt less.

We have heard "ignorance is bliss," and we are tempted to judge and criticize ignorant people. Yet there is a form of ignorance that serves us well, and that is ignorance of limiting beliefs. In a *Calvin and Hobbes* cartoon, Calvin declares: "It's not denial. I'm just selective about the reality I accept." Every reality is available to us, right now — including realities far more wondrous than the one we currently live in. To step into them, however, we must drop our self-limiting beliefs.

When I wrote my first book, *The Dragon Doesn't Live Here Anymore*, I was blissfully ignorant about writing and the publishing industry. I wrote for the sheer delight of expressing myself, and I published the book myself. Within a few months the book became popular, and before long I was reprinting in quantities of 10,000 and traveling around the world to present seminars.

Then one day I walked into a bookstore where my book was being sold, and I was appalled at the huge number of books on similar subject matters—they took up nearly a whole wall! Suddenly it occurred to me that if I had walked into the store and seen all the good books already presented in my field, I would have felt intimidated and probably never set pen to paper. But I was ignorant—and that made all the difference.

Later, as I got to know the publishing industry, I learned

all the rules: what kinds of books sell, covers that attract attention, agents who can influence publishers, hooks to appeal to various markets, and so on. In retrospect, I am very glad I didn't know the rules, because most of the rules lead to the disappointing conclusion that only a small percentage of writers will succeed. Some of the other writers who didn't know the rules were Dale Carnegie, Norman Vincent Peale, and James Redfield. Is there a message here?

Back in 1951, running a four-minute mile was considered by many to be physiologically impossible. Then Roger Bannister ran the mile in 3:59.4. Within six months, forty other contenders beat the unbeatable limit. Did they all find a crate of the same vitamins? No, they all found the same new belief system. When Roger Bannister broke the four-minute barrier, it was a mental barrier, not a physical one.

A number of years ago in Australia, a 61-year-old farmer named Cliff Young entered a grueling 400-kilometer race wearing coveralls and galoshes. As the younger, well-trained athletes laughed, Cliff went on to win the race in record time—a full day and a half before competitors forty years his junior. How did Cliff do the impossible? Nobody told him he was supposed to sleep.

The word *impossible* begins with an "imp." Get the imp out of your vision, and you will step into a world of un-limited possibilities. Do not ask life to shrink to fit your beliefs; expand your beliefs to include all that life has to offer. Swami Satchidananda explains: "We started out fine. Then we got de-fined. Now we need to get re-fined."

Children are the happiest people on the planet because

they have not learned what they cannot do. They have not been taught to fear and judge and hate, and they have no concept that they must justify their existence by hard work. Lord, please keep me ignorant, so I may remember my innocence and see the world as You created it.

For Reflection

1. Can you remember a time in your life when you believed you could be or do or have anything you wanted? Describe your attitude at that time and the feelings that accompanied it.

2. What do you enjoy about being in the presence of children or animals? What lessons might they be offering you?

3. Is there anything you would like to do that you believe you cannot do? Would you be willing to reconsider your belief? Can you find evidence that you *can* do it?

Soul Required

*E*very frazzled traveler waiting for the airport shuttle van needed to get somewhere quickly, and each one considered his or her need most important. The heat of the day didn't help. The driver, a fortyish African-American fellow, stocky with a bit of stubble on his chin, was doing his best to move the passengers onto the van. As he passed by, I glimpsed his name badge. It said "Doug." I didn't envy Doug that morning.

The final passenger to board the van was an Asian woman with a splint on her knee. Doug had saved two seats by the door for her and her young son, about six years old. In contrast to the frenzy around him, Doug took the time to gently help the woman into her place. Carefully, he set her leg on a little stool; then he turned to the boy, who was still standing outside the van, and he had a heart-to-heart talk with him: "You know your momma needs you now, don't you?"

The child silently nodded.

"She's counting on you to help her. Now you 'de man,' you understand?"

Again the boy nodded. Doug gave him a friendly pat on the rear and lovingly lifted him onto the seat next to his mom.

Doug slid the side door shut, took his driver's seat, and got the vehicle rolling. My mind, however, was still at the curbside. I had just witnessed an act of extraordinary caring. In the midst of a sea of confusion and self-centeredness, this humble man had deftly taken care of God's business.

The world teaches us that greatness equals scads of bucks in the bank, celebrity fame, movie-star looks, or power over others. But there is one measure of greatness that exceeds them all: *kindness.*

Jesus told the parable of a successful man who spent all his time building barns to store the goods he had accumulated. Then, the story goes, one night God chastised the man. "You fool!" exclaimed God. "This very night your soul will be required, and who will get what you have stored up?"

In some Bible translations, "your soul will be required" is translated as "you are going to die." I, however, interpret the phrase literally: "Tonight you will be called to be fully present, with your soul fully alive." The lesson is not a threat of death, but an invitation to life.

At every moment, your soul is required. You have probably had the experience of being on a date or at a business meeting with someone whose spirit was not present. You likely felt frustrated, confused, or ripped off; you wanted to connect with the person and he or she was not there. You were hungry to feel his or her spirit, just as the world is hungry to feel yours. Soul is the active ingredient that makes a life worthwhile, bestowing joy wherever it shines.

One morning when I arrived at the Miami airport after traveling all night, I was quite tired and I didn't feel well.

I walked into a coffee shop and ordered some orange juice. The waitress, a jovial Hispanic woman who probably had children, put down her order pad and asked me: "Is that all you're having, sweetie? Why don't you have something substantial for breakfast?" I swear she was channeling my Jewish mother!

I felt very touched. Here in the midst of a very impersonal airport, with thousands of people of many cultures and languages milling around chaotically, this dear woman took a personal interest in me. Suddenly I felt better. "Yes, I think I will have a bagel," I told her. And was it delicious! When her soul showed up, so did mine.

Perhaps the aphorism of Jesus most apropos today is, "What shall it profit a man if he gains the whole world, but loses his soul?" Never before have so many people had access to the whole world, and never before have so many lost their souls in the process. Many successful people are materially nourished yet spiritually emaciated. How rare and wonderful it is to meet someone who has climbed the corporate ladder and still has a light in the eyes that says: "I am here. Are you?"

My friend Kristi Peterson is a producer for CNN in Atlanta. Kristi took me on an insider's tour of the facility and introduced me to many of the producers and technicians. Everyone was busy. Some were manic. A few bordered on being fried. Finally, Kristi took me to the office of the president of CNN Domestic, Jim Walton. Jim oversees all CNN TV channels in the United States and all CNN's English Web sites. Considering this man's position and responsibilities, I expected our meeting to be quick and impersonal. To my surprise, Jim was the most present and spiritually available person in the facility. I felt his heart in his handshake. He really looked me in the eye. He seemed genuinely open to meet me. We had a real conversation. I was quite impressed, even touched, by Jim's energetic availability. He taught me that it is possible to be in a position of immense worldly authority and still keep one's soul alive.

If you have given your soul away, eventually you want nothing more than to get it back. Without your spirit, you have nothing; with it, you have everything. I remember a seminar participant who, during an exercise, realized that he had given his life away to please other people. His realization was so deep that it brought him to almost violent tears. I remember his wailing at the top of his lungs: "I want my life back! I just want my life back!"

In that moment, he retrieved it. When you really want your soul back, you get it. But you must want your soul more than anything you are enticed to trade it for. Then it is really yours. In truth, you can never really lose your soul. You can lose touch with it, but you cannot lose it. Your soul is the one thing that is yours forever, for you are an expression of God, and God is eternal. The soul game is not so much about keeping or losing it, but remembering it as you go.

Every now and then someone shows up who reminds us that life is not about getting somewhere. It is about being somewhere. Like Doug, the van driver. Maybe I can be like him when I grow up.

For Reflection

1. Who is the most soulfully alive person you know? What do you feel in his or her presence? Why do you enjoy being with him or her?

2. Have you ever traded your soul for something you wanted? What did you discover? How did you get your soul back?

3. During how much of today has your soul been present? How much of every day? What can you do to keep it with you more?

The True Perfectionist

A friend of mine told me: "I used to think I was a perfectionist. I found the tiniest flaws in everything. Then I realized I was not a perfectionist at all; I was an imperfectionist. If I were a perfectionist, I would see perfection wherever I look."

The life we experience is a result of the vision we choose. At any moment we can see through the eyes of appreciation or of criticism. And we will see more of whatever we are focusing on. We master the game of life by finding opportunity where others see dead ends. Then we discover opportunity everywhere.

While having lunch with some business associates at an upscale restaurant, one of our party asked the waiter for an unusual dish not on the menu. The waiter replied that he would ask the chef if he could prepare the dish. Then another member of our group sarcastically commented, "I'll bet that will just make the chef's day!"

But the waiter did not flinch. "Actually," he replied smoothly, "I'm sure he will be glad to accommodate you—this gives him a chance to shine."

Every situation gives us a chance to shine, if we recognize our power as creative spirits. No situation is any one

way, except what we make it. *You can make anything out of anything.* So why not make it perfect?

Imagine a man walking along a city street when a flowerpot falls off a sill above him, misses hitting him by inches, and crashes at his feet. There are four paths of response the man might take. First, the path of *knee-jerk reaction*: he would yell a curse toward the window or perhaps dash up the stairs, find the owner, and punch him out. Second, the path of *the victim*: this experience would confirm his belief that the world is out to get him, and he would go about the rest of his day (or life) protecting himself from evil, retelling his story many times. Third, the path of *detachment*: he would rationalize that this was his karma, do nothing, and just keep walking. Finally, the path of *love*: he would go to the flower store on the corner, buy a new plant, and deliver it to the person whose plant had been blown off the sill by the wind.

The world is not defective and does not need fixing; the world is unfolding and needs belief. You will never create a perfect world by fixing everything that is broken. The more things or people you try to fix, the more you find that are broken. The only way to attain perfection is to claim it right where you are. If it is not here now, it will not be here later. Perfection is not a condition you attain; it is a consciousness you live from. Changing the world is not about *setting* it right, but *seeing* it right. Inner transformation must occur before outer change is possible.

Ram Dass noted that there are three kinds of people: those who say, "not enough!"; those who say, "too much!"; and those who say, "ah, just right!" Actually, there are just two kinds of people, for "too much" of one thing is really "not enough" of another. Every moment is a choice between resistance and affirmation.

Does seeing perfection mean we are to be passive observers and sit around and do nothing? Not at all. Perfection includes the process of changing, growing, expanding, improving, and moving ahead. But our actions to improve do not proceed from an attitude of pushing against lack. They proceed from a sense that things are already good, and wouldn't it be a delightful adventure to make them better? The true perfectionist creates effective change by seeing the highest possibilities and becoming so excited about them that conditions must transform to match the vision.

Several years ago while I was walking through the Los Angeles airport, I felt annoyed by the massive construction going on around me. I saw temporary plywood walls to my left and right, a row of huge scaffolds, and long detours to baggage claim. I grumbled to myself about what a mess the place was and how long it was taking to fix it. Then I came upon a poster that stopped me in my tracks. It was an artist's rendering of what the airport would look like when the construction was complete. And magnificent it was! The glass atrium roofs, sleek marbled corridors, and potted palms were a delight to behold—a far cry from the current mess. Then I relaxed. If that is what this is leading to, I thought, then I am glad they are doing it. As I dropped my resistance, I enjoyed the entire process, including the construction phase.

The entire universe is in a construction phase, never

totally complete as it is, but always perfect in the process. When you appreciate the magic as you go, you become a true perfectionist.

For Reflection

1. Do you have any pet peeves you regularly grumble about? Do you notice that the more you grumble about them, the more they show up in your experiences?

2. Do you believe that the world is broken and needs fixing? How does that feel? Experiment with the attitude that life is perfect as it is, always in the process of becoming more conscious, colorful, and rewarding. Notice how that feels and how effective you become as a result.

3. Can you remember a time when, as William James described, "the doors of perception were cleansed," and you recognized the perfection of life?

How to Goof Off

*I*signed up with a trash removal service that requires rural customers to mark their addresses on their garbage cans. I took a can of white spray paint and etched my street number on one of the brown rubber cans. I set the can in the back of my SUV, drove it to the end of my road, and left the garbage in the appropriate spot. When I returned to my garage, I was irked to notice that some of the white paint had rubbed off on the back of my seat; apparently, it had not fully dried on the can. But it did dry on my car. I tried to remove the paint, but by that time it was stuck fast.

Over the next weeks and months, every time I noticed the paint marks on the back of the seat, I felt foolish; a stream of judgment chided me: "If you had paid closer attention and left more time for the paint to dry, this wouldn't have happened. Now you have ruined your car seat, and every time you look at it, you are to be reminded of your carelessness." (Do you know that voice?)

Then one day I accompanied a friend to the local hardware store to find some paint. On a shelf I noticed a small can called Goof Off—a remover of paint and other hard-to-get-out stains. I grabbed a can, took it home, and applied it to the defiant stain. To my delight, the paint disappeared instantly!

I now see this product—especially its name—as symbolic of forgiveness. The name acknowledges that you made a mistake ("goof")—but it also acknowledges that it can be undone ("off"). If you are subject to the tyranny of guilt, this name offers an especially important teaching: Any sin is forgivable. Any error is correctable. Nothing is etched in stone. You always have another chance.

A Course in Miracles distinguishes between a sin and an error: a sin requires punishment, but an error simply requires correction. The *Course* goes on to tell us that we have made many errors, but we have never sinned. All our sins ("self-inflicted nonsense") are undone the moment we bring our judgmental thoughts into the healing light of love.

The story is told about a Filipino woman named Josephine who claimed to have daily conversations with Jesus. A cynical priest heard about Josephine and sought to debunk her. He went to her and asked, "Is it true that you talk to Jesus every day?"

"Yes, I do," she answered.

"Then the next time you talk to Jesus, would you ask him what sin I committed when I was in the seminary?" the priest asked smugly. Then he walked away proudly, certain he had cornered the charlatan and would soon expose her.

A week later the priest returned to Josephine and asked her, "Did you ask Jesus what my sin was?"

"Yes, I did," she answered.

"And what did he say?" asked the priest.

"He said, 'I forgot.'"

There is no sin so heinous that it cannot be undone by reframing it in compassion. Love has no consciousness of our sins; God sees us only as pure and innocent. It is *we* who have fabricated the concept of sin and crushed our life force under it. *A Course in Miracles* also tells us, "God does not forgive because He never has condemned." In the inspiring movie *Brother Sun, Sister Moon,* the Pope tells St. Francis, "In our obsession with Original Sin, we have overlooked Original Innocence."

All self-judgment can be undone by recognizing that we have never committed a crime against God. I met a man who, during his senior year in college, was walking past the college bookstore where he saw a large display of yearbooks on the sidewalk outside. Since this fellow had no money, he grabbed a book and kept walking. Over the next few days he began to feel guilty about his theft, and he decided to return the book and confess. He went to the bookstore manager and guiltily admitted, "I stole this book."

The manager told him, "Come with me." Then he led the student to the yearbook display and pointed to a sign the young man had not seen: "Free—Please take one."

I am not suggesting you go out and steal anything or hurt anyone. This true story serves as a metaphor: For every sin you can find in your life, God can find a way to forgive it. For every way you have separated yourself from love, higher consciousness reminds you that you have never for a moment been outside of grace. And for every paint stain you berate yourself for leaving, there is a can of Goof Off to remove it.

For Reflection

1. Are you still condemning yourself for a mistake you made in the past? What did you do, and how do you feel about it now?

2. How do you think a loving God regards this act?

3. Can you find a way to reframe your experience with compassion so that you no longer feel guilty? If someone else came to you and said that he or she had done the same thing, what might be your response?

Let Me Help You Remember

While exiting a grocery store, I noticed an unusual poster announcing: "You already know how to meditate. Let me help you remember." Ah, what an empowering offer—a sharp contrast to the many advertisements for products and services that tell us we are wanting and needing salvation.

How wonderful it feels—and how powerfully it works—to regard ourselves and one another as innately wise, capable of accomplishing anything we choose and greater than any challenge before us. Wouldn't you like to be regarded as magnificent?

A few years ago I signed up for a "You Fly" airplane flight, which promised that I would be able to take the stick of a small airplane and control the plane myself. Flying an airplane has been one of my longtime dreams, so I eagerly registered for the flight, a three-hour jaunt over three Hawaiian islands. What a thrill, I imagined, to be in control of the aircraft for a few minutes in midair!

On the appointed day, I drove to the Maui airport, where I met the pilot, Scott. I informed Scott that I had never piloted a plane before, and he told me that would be no problem. Scott led me out on the tarmac to a small twin-engine Cessna, where he gave me a brief rundown

about the various instruments on the control panel. Scott strapped himself into the seat next to mine and told me, "Now here's how you take off . . ."

Excuse me, I thought; I don't remember the advertisement saying anything about taking off. I started to open my mouth to say, "Perhaps you didn't hear me say that I've never flown before." But when I looked over at Scott, he was on the radio setting up our takeoff with the control tower. Suddenly I understood what was happening: he thought I could do it. To Scott, taking off was not too much to ask of me. So, in spite of my hesitation, I decided to keep my mouth shut. I figured that if I had a choice between Scott's being right about my ability to take off and my being right about my inability, I would rather choose his opinion. I would rather fulfill his expectation of my greatness than my expectation of my ineptitude. I decided to believe in his belief. I followed Scott's careful instructions, and within a few minutes we were airborne.

I flew the airplane nearly three hours that day. I flew over the dramatic north shore of Maui, past the thousand-foot sweeping verdant cliffs of Molokai, across the golden sand beaches of Lanai, then over whales and dolphins cavorting in the azure ocean channel back to Maui. There we buzzed my house and made our way back to the airport. For nearly all that time, I controlled the airplane, with Scott stepping in occasionally to make minor corrections. My nervousness had given way to exhilaration, my doubts to confidence.

As we approached the airport, Scott surprised me again. "Now here's how you land," he told me in a nonchalant way. *Now wait just a minute*, I felt like saying, à la Barney

Fife. Taking off and flying is one thing, but landing—now that's outright *dangerous*. Then I remembered a lesson from one of my favorite flyers, Richard Bach, who suggested, "Argue for your limits, and sure enough they're yours." I kept my mouth shut.

As I guided the plane in according to Scott's instructions, the Cessna was rocked by a gust of wind. "Sure is windy here," Scott laughed. "I've seen pilots who got their licenses on the mainland come here and try to deal with these trade winds and suddenly realize they didn't really know how to land." *Yow!* Okay, just breathe, I thought. I kept following Scott's directions until he took over the stick just before touchdown.

As I left the airport that day, I felt higher than our flight. Scott's belief in me brought out the best in me. The airplane flight lasted three hours; the lesson was for a lifetime.

Then I remembered the compelling film *Stand and Deliver*, in which Edward James Olmos dramatized the true story of Jaime Escalante, a math teacher who went into the Los Angeles *barrios* and decided to teach calculus to some of the school's lowest-functioning students. When the math department chairwoman criticized Jaime, he boldly told her, "The students will rise to the level of the teacher's expectations!" Everyone in Jaime's class went on to pass the state calculus test.

At any given moment we have two voices in our heads: one that tells us we can't, and another that tells us we can. Which will prove true? The one you give the most attention to. The one you act on. The one you make a stand for.

You already know how to be magnificent. Let me help you remember.

For Reflection

1. Have you ever experienced a contrast between what you thought you could do and someone else's greater belief in you? How did that person's vision of your possibilities help bring forth your power?

2. What kinds of "rewards" or "payoffs" do people receive from thinking or acting small? Are these truly rewards, or is there a grander reward for thinking large?

3. Consider any situations in your life in which you are arguing for your limits. What argument can you make for your possibilities?

Table With a View

*J*ust as I was settling into my afternoon beach reverie, I was jarred by a deep voice: "Excuse me, sir, we are going to need this spot." I looked up, brushed the sand from my cheek, and gazed at a young man wearing a debonair waiter's tuxedo, his head crowned by the palm tree swaying behind him. He bore an air of authority.

Okay, okay. Groggily I picked up my towel, moved ten yards to the left, and watched him and an assistant set up a small dining table on the grassy hillside. They laid a fine, white linen across the tabletop and set out exquisite cutlery, as if the scene were overlooking not the beach, but the San Francisco skyline.

"Is there some kind of party happening?" I asked.

"It's a wedding anniversary."

"How many people are you preparing for?"

"Two."

"Two?"

"Yes, it's a couple's twenty-fifth anniversary. The husband is surprising his wife with a private catered dinner overlooking the beach."

I stayed and watched. An hour later, on a verdant knoll overlooking Wailea Beach in Maui, a gray-templed man and his wife, both dressed in fine aloha attire, strolled along, hand in hand. As they approached the chic table and dapper waiter with a linen napkin draped professionally over his arm, the husband casually motioned to his wife and asked her, "Why don't we sit here, sweetheart?" She returned his nudge with astonishment. Then he pulled a chair back for her. She hesitated, wondering if this was some kind of joke, but then she took her seat, utterly perplexed. Then a handful of attendants emerged from behind the bushes and proceeded to serve the anniversary couple a five-course meal fit for a king and queen—before one of the most spectacular backdrops on the planet.

Let's hear it for romance, folks.

Passion is a sacred experience. It is the very spark of life, the spirit-stream that animates everything that lives. Passion keeps the force of evolution eternally on its cutting edge. It is the hand of God reaching into humanity to elevate it to divinity.

The film *Sirens* suggests that we do not need to wait until we die to go to heaven. We can meet God right here on Earth. The film, based on a true story, follows an uptight nineteenth-century Anglican priest and his stuffy wife as they travel to Australia, where they have been dispatched by the church to mend the evil ways of a painter who has attained notoriety for drawing nudes. When the couple arrives at the painter's compound, they find him surrounded with a sumptuous array of sensual delights, including supple women who run nude on the grounds. The Anglicans are aghast and set out to reform the evildoers. As time goes on, however, the couple learns to appreciate the painter's artistic vision and his passion for life. Eventually the preacher and his wife are transformed as they discover the hand of God in the midst of the world. Instead of convincing the painter he is a sinner, they deepen their knowledge of love. While they set out to shut down his heart, he sets theirs on fire.

Hawaiian musician Jay Larrin sings a marvelous song, "Don't Let the Song Go Out of Your Life." Jay's music reflects some important questions asked by shamanistic author Angeles Arrien: "When did you stop singing? When did you stop dancing? When did you grow uncomfortable with the sweet territory of silence? When did you stop being enchanted by stories?"

In one way or another, we have all sold out on our passions. Perhaps at an early age we traded our joys for approval, acceptance, and societal security. We did not realize that true security comes not from hiding out in dogma, but stepping out with love.

It is never too late to have a happy childhood. While we may have stifled our passions, we can never extinguish them. At any moment we can reclaim our dreams and start to live as if our lives depend on it. Then we become master painters, with all life the canvas.

Real romance is not limited to sunset dinners and rollicking sex. True romance is a zeal we bring to everything we do. We can bring passion to our careers, families, ideas, and spiritual lives. Indeed, what is more spiritual than fire in the soul?

We are ripe for a passion revolution. If you fear passion, you deny your purpose. If you embrace passion, you stay true to your destiny. When you bring romance to life, you enroll everyone you touch. Why settle for a stuffy restaurant when you can have dinner on the beach?

For Reflection

1. When was the last time you did something on the spur of the moment, simply for sheer delight? How did it feel?

2. On a scale of 1-10, how much passion do you feel in your work? Your relationship? Your body? Your home? Your friendships? Your spiritual path? Any other aspect of your life?

3. What could you do today for a friend, lover, or colleague as a spontaneous expression of love?

Sleeping for World Peace

*W*hen I telephoned my friend John one afternoon, his wife answered the phone. "John isn't available at the moment," she told me. "He's sleeping for world peace."

Sleeping for world peace. Hmmm. Has sort of a nice ring to it. Maybe it's a practice worth cultivating.

Sometimes the most powerful action you can take toward solving a problem is to step back and let it go for the moment. Allow the wisdom of nature to take its course. If you try to force a situation when you are feeling afraid, angry, confused, victimized, or self-righteous, you will not be effective (and probably have to retrace your steps to make corrections). If, on the other hand, you regroup and find your center before taking action, you will be bolstered by authentic power. As Buddha might have said, "Don't just do something—stand there."

Ram Dass underscored the importance of the energy we imbue in our actions. "You may be marching for world peace," he suggests, "but if you are immersed in anger, hatred, or divisiveness, you are sending out a set of vibrations that is just causing more war."

I saw a demonstration of this principle during the 1970s when I was involved in the antiwar movement. In my

73

hometown there were several activist groups, and none of them got anywhere. They were fighting with one another and within their own ranks. How could they expect to end war on the planet when they couldn't even get along together? From that experience I learned that my foremost responsibility is not to save the entire world, but to remain centered and do my best to generate peace in my sphere of daily influence. Then I, like you, can receive an M.B.U. degree—and become a Mobile Blessing Unit.

Manifesting peace, personally and globally, follows four steps: (1) get a clear vision of what you want to create; (2) find and cultivate the feeling of already having it; (3) act when you are peaceful, centered, and confident; and then (4) let go and allow the Universe to handle the details.

If you need to handle any details in the process, the Universe will give you clear instructions. If not, don't butt into God's business. Many important projects are thwarted by underacting, but just as many are thwarted by overacting. Yes, you must do, and yes, you must also allow.

For many of us who have been taught that everything depends on our actions, allowing can be more of a challenge than doing—yet it may be the crucial element to achieve a success that has been eluding us. Doing is necessary, but *being* is crucial. As a spiritual being, the spirit you bring to your actions has a far deeper and broader effect than anxious labor.

Arnold Patent, author of *You Can Have It All,* suggests, "If you ever feel that you should do something, lie down until the feeling passes." There are two basic positions from which we may act: If you work from *obligation*, you will be resentful, tired, and ineffective. If you proceed from *inspiration*, you will be joyful, achieve success, and have unlimited energy to create and serve.

One day I was looking for a document I needed to resolve a financial snafu. When I could not find it, I became agitated and stepped up my search to a feverish pace. Eventually I realized I was getting nowhere. Then an inner voice prompted me, "Just sit down, relax, and clear your mind." I stepped back from my search and took a few minutes to meditate. As I was enjoying my state of peace, an image popped into my mind, showing me the rear section of a particular file cabinet drawer. When I finished my meditation, I went to the drawer and immediately found the document I needed.

Good artists and graphic designers will tell you that the space in a painting or written page is as important as the colors or words. In the same way, we must make space for our spirit to breathe in the midst of our activities. Observe dogs, cats, birds, and other animals in their natural states: they nap frequently and refresh their spirits as they go. Great geniuses recognize and make use of this important habit. Henry Ford and Albert Einstein, for example, were known for taking twenty-minute catnaps during their workdays. Ultimately they became two of the most prolific and monumental contributors to cultural and scientific progress in the twentieth century.

I know a fellow who serves as an efficiency consultant to large corporations. He teaches the power of "creative loafing." One high-level executive, after taking my friend's course, decided to take one day off of work each week for play, creativity, and spiritual renewal. After a few months of the practice, he reported that the ideas he came up with on his play day, coupled with his soul refreshment, yielded far more success than he had been achieving by plugging along in his daily grind.

When we sleep deeply, we enjoy direct communion with our spiritual nature and our soul abides in peace. Significant physical, emotional, and mental healing occurs during sleep—renewal that we do not obtain when we are immersed in the activities of the world. No kidding, sleeping may ultimately be your greatest contribution to world peace.

For Reflection

1. Do you take time each day to nurture your spirit? What activities refresh your soul and inspire you to greater creativity?

2. Do you feel stuck or bogged down on a project you are currently working on? Is it possible you are trying too hard? Can you step back and let the project go for a while and do something to renew yourself?

3. Do you know anyone who works in a relaxed way, yet gets a lot accomplished? Why do you think this person is successful?

Stronger Than Hope

*I*set out with a group of friends on a sailboat excursion to camp on the mystical island of Molokai. Just before our ship reached harbor, we were overtaken by a blustering tropical storm; all we could do for an hour was tread water amidst huge, churning swells. Quite a few of our retinue made trips to the rail, and by the time the squall abated and we reached shore, numerous would-be sailors had waxed, green faces and swore to take the plane next time.

Fortunately, the weather improved and we went on to enjoy a luscious retreat on a white-sand beach sloping into a crystalline lagoon. The following day as we prepared to leave the island, several in our group felt anxious about the prospect of hitting bad weather again. Someone suggested we gather for a group prayer for easy passage. So we assembled on the beach, held hands, and visualized a smooth, relaxed trip. I spoke a strong affirmation that *wherever we go, God is, and all is well.* By the time we finished praying, the group's apprehension had lifted and we came into a sense of positive expectation.

The moment we opened our eyes, a young man in our midst, unfamiliar with the practice of prayer, blurted out, "Yeah, and let's hope we don't hit any more storms!"

Bonk! His statement crashed awkwardly against the

vision we had just created. Afterward, I took the fellow aside and gently explained to him an important principle.

Once you have prayed for something, you must step fully into the consciousness of what you have prayed for, and not backpedal into thoughts, words, or actions that reinforce the condition you were praying to heal. You are always affirming what you want or what you don't want, and everything you think, say, or do is directing your energy in one direction or another. Our words and actions after a prayer must continue to uphold the prayer, not refute it. Prayer is not something you do once, and it is a done deal; it is a consciousness you establish that becomes a foundation for all future experiences.

When I was studying with master healer Hilda Charlton, we prayed during a class for a woman who was seeking to be healed of a particular disease. After the prayer session, a man approached the woman and suggested she try a certain herbal treatment. At the following week's class, Hilda vehemently admonished the fellow and the group: "How dare you undo the healing work we did! We spent a long time and a lot of energy bringing this woman into the consciousness of wholeness—and you speak to her as if she needs help! If she is not sick, as we declared her to be, why would you tell her what to do to erase her illness? If you are participating in a prayer, don't you dare undo it!"

Hilda was not against medicine (on many occasions she recommended that students take it), and she was extremely compassionate with people who were suffering. Hilda was using the incident to underscore an important point, one which has helped me immensely over many years: To be an effective healer, speak to the place in your clients that is whole, and treat people as if they are already who they would like to be. The greatest gift you can offer people is your vision of their well-being. As Richard Bach suggests in *Jonathan Livingston Seagull,* "Begin by knowing that you've already arrived."

In a famous biblical story, God advised Lot and his family to leave Sodom because the city was about to be destroyed. God told the family to leave quickly and not look back. On their road to freedom, Lot's wife turned to see what was happening behind her, and she immediately turned into a pillar of salt. Certainly this event did not happen literally—the story is a metaphor, a grand piece of advice for all times: Don't get involved with what you are leaving behind. Your past may be laden with pain, suffering, and hardship, but you are building a new life. Leave the past where it was, and turn your attention fully toward where you are heading. As Jesus advised, "Let the dead bury their dead."

Springtime is a metaphor for new birth. Our religions celebrate spring with important holidays. In Judaism, we commemorate Passover, representing the ascension from slavery to freedom. In Christianity, we celebrate the resurrection of Christ. The full moon of May is considered Buddha's birthday. When celebrating these holidays, we must remember to concentrate on forward movement. We have paid far too much attention to scenes of slavery and crucifixion; we have played them out time and again. Now it is time for us to focus on what happens next. The more we rehash how we got where we are, the more we stay where we were. The more we analyze what is not work-

ing, the more things do not work. And the more we consider how we would like our lives to be, the more things become as we would have them.

Real spirituality is beyond hope. Hope means there is a chance things *may* turn out as we wish, and if we are lucky we *may* get what we want. Faith, on the other hand, firmly maintains the awareness that love is present now, well-being is our natural state, and all really is well.

Yes, we may have hit a storm on the way over, but that does not mean we have to hit one on the way back.

For Reflection

1. Are there any past dramas in your life that you keep recounting, mentally or verbally? How do you feel when you repeat them? Try putting yourself on a history fast for thirty days. Do not tell any old stories or talk about conditions you are trying to end. Notice how you feel during and at the conclusion of the fast.

2. When someone comes to you with a problem, practice seeing him or her as whole and capable of handling the challenge deftly. Notice the results of regarding the person in this light.

3. Call to mind any situations in which you feel afraid, insecure, or vulnerable. Then take the affirmation: *Wherever I am, God is, and all is well.* Keep applying the affirmation until you feel a sense of relief, safety, and well-being.

Blessed Be the Cage Rattlers

*W*hen I arrived home after a long trip, I discovered that a rat had been marauding my pantry. I set a Have-a-Heart trap, and within a few days caught the fuzzy intruder. Naturally, the anxious rodent didn't like being trapped in the cage and scurried about in a frenzy to try to find his way out. Several hours later I took the rat out to a field to release him, and there he taught me a powerful lesson.

As I tilted the cage and opened the door for the critter to slide out, to my surprise, he did not jump out. Instead, he clung to the cage for dear life. The more I shook the cage to dislodge him, the tighter he grasped the wire mesh that entrapped him. Finally, I gave the cage a good shake, and out he slid. Quickly he scurried to freedom.

It occurred to me that we humans act something like the rat when our cages are being rattled. We create traps of addiction, abusive relationships, and meaningless jobs, and then we cling to these unhealthful situations as if they were our salvation. We complain about our cages, assert that we are stuck because of someone else's fault, and fantasize about being free; but after a while we get used to our cages and even feel a sense of familiarity and safety there. Then, when our world is shaken up, we rail and com-

plain as if something terrible is being thrust upon us. What we do not realize, in that moment, is that we are being given a chance to break free.

The Jewish commentary on the Bible tells that when the Hebrew slaves were released from bondage in Egypt, they found themselves in a vast wilderness. During trying times, many in the new nation shouted, "Let's go back to Egypt—at least we were assured of food and shelter there!" What they forgot, in their moment of insecurity, was why they left in the first place. They forgot that they had been slaves and were seeking a greater life. Similarly, when African-Americans were released from slavery after the Emancipation Proclamation, a certain number chose to return to indentured service voluntarily. The freedom and responsibility to create a life of their own choosing seemed too much for them to bear.

We may not be slaves to political tyrants, but we may still cling to our old lives as a source of security. The voice of fear beguiles us: "Maintain the known at all costs—even if the known stinks." For some reason, the familiar seems more attractive than the unknown, even though the opportunity at our doorstep offers us infinitely more than what we have settled for. At such a time we do well to take a deep breath, remember *why* we are moving ahead, and just keep walking. Eventually the Hebrews did arrive at the Promised Land, and so does every individual or group that holds the vision and perseveres.

At a retreat I conducted, a woman came to me each day with critical observations about the program. She was a corporate efficiency expert who had been trained to find things wrong and make suggestions how to correct them. When she first approached me, I felt offended and became a bit defensive. After the second and third days, however, I began to listen to what she was saying. I realized that she had some really good ideas! At that moment I recognized she was on my team, and there was no need to take her criticisms personally. Ultimately, she attended several more programs and we became friends.

Sometimes people rattle our cages when they are simply upset, and they are not offering us any real constructive criticism. This scenario offers us different gifts. Can you hold your peace in the face of another's anger or judgment? Can you, as Rudyard Kipling eloquently stated, "keep your head when all about you are losing theirs and blaming it on you"? If you can, you are well on your way to spiritual mastery. It is easy to be at peace when others around you are approving of you. If you can hold your peace when someone has gone bonkers, you can truly claim peace as your own.

Do you remember Kato in the *Pink Panther* movies? Inspector Clouseau would come home in the evening, for example, and Kato would jump out of a closet and attack him. The two would exchange martial arts blows for a while, until Clouseau pinned Kato. Then Clouseau would thank him. Kato, you see, was Clouseau's houseboy. His job was to try to catch the inspector off guard, so Clouseau could keep himself fit and his skills sharp.

When Jesus performed one of his healings, he declared, "This is not sickness unto death, but for the glory of God." We can say this, as well, of our cage rattlers; they are not here to destroy us, but to empower us. We must reframe our challenges to discover how the Universe is

trying to pry us loose from an old situation that does not work for us. Thank the Universe for the people and situations that challenge you, for, seen correctly, they are not keeping you in bondage, but assisting you to be released from it.

For Reflection

1. Can you recall a time in your life when you felt utterly disoriented, as if your very foundation was being shaken out from under you? Were there blessings that happened as a result?

2. Do you feel attracted to returning to any old situations that brought you pain? Why do you think you feel drawn back? What do you think would happen if you returned?

3. Can you think of someone who has challenged you, yet ultimately helped you?

The Complete Genius

*W*hile meandering through a bookstore, I discovered a wealth of books for dummies and idiots. You have probably seen the many volumes directed at stupid people, such as *Computers for Dummies* and *The Total Nerd's Guide to Fitness*. I even saw *The Complete Idiot's Guide to Out-of-Body Experiences!* There are hundreds of titles in each of these very popular series, with the number growing rapidly.

I was struck by how readily we identify ourselves as dummies and idiots. Obviously, we think we are stupid, and these books will help. I wonder what would happen if I published a similar series for geniuses, such as *Golf for Sages* or *The Complete Genius's Guide to Home Repair.* I have a hunch they wouldn't sell very well at all. Not because we are not geniuses. Because we have been trained to regard ourselves as stupid.

When I was a little boy, I sat on my front porch one morning and sang to myself several rousing verses of "Take Me Out to the Ball Game." A few days later I overheard my mother casually tell her friend, "Alan has a foghorn voice." That idea made an impression on me, and I did not sing for many years. After all (at that age), your

mother knows everything, and if she said I couldn't sing, I couldn't sing.

Perhaps you had a similar experience. Perhaps early in your life someone said or did something unkind to you, and you adopted a self-image that defined you as small, ugly, incapable, or unlovable. Most of us did. And perhaps you went on to live as if that identity were true. And perhaps, like many, you accumulated a deep-seated pool of unwept tears in your soul and you went through life hurting because you wished you could be more.

You *are* more. The genius you were born as still lives and can be reactivated at any moment. Genius is your reality, and the dark programming is your adopted personality. When the spiritual teacher Abraham (through Esther Hicks) was challenged, "You can't teach an old dog new tricks," Abraham responded, "You have no idea what an old dog you are!" Who you were before you learned self-defeating patterns is still very much available and eager to come forth and shine.

There is a story in the annals of education about an elementary school teacher who arrived on the first day of school and perused her class roster. Next to each child's name was the number of a very high IQ: "126 ... 134 ... 140," Miss Everett read aloud, eyebrows raised. "Thank goodness I finally got a bright class!"

Miss Everett went on to stimulate the loftiest abilities in her whiz kids. She assigned them challenging projects, took them on field trips, and offered them freedom to explore their work in creative ways. At the end of the semester, as she expected, all the students earned As and Bs. The day after report cards were issued, the principal called the teacher into his office and asked, "Miss Everett, what did you do with these kids?"

"What do you mean?" asked the teacher innocently.

"You took some of the lowest-functioning students in the school and turned them into geniuses!"

"I don't understand what you're talking about," she replied. "These children were bright when I got them. Here, just look at their IQs in my roll book."

The principal scanned her roster and, astonished, replied, "Miss Everett, these are their locker numbers!"

The people around us tend to become who we think they are, so let us focus on the highest in everyone we meet. Renowned success teacher Dale Carnegie, author of the popular self-help book, *How to Win Friends and Influence People,* began his career in an unexpected way. One night while he was teaching an adult-school English course, Carnegie ran out of lecture material before the class time was over. So he invited several students to each stand before the class and talk about him- or herself—an exercise utterly unheard of at that time. The results were extraordinary! The students came to life in ways far more compelling than when they were studying English. And the class responded enthusiastically! Carnegie happened upon the transformational power of authentic self-expression, which ultimately revolutionized (perhaps even created) the field of personal development. Later he wrote, "Give them a reputation to live up to!"

The words *genius* and *genuine* are almost identical, and they proceed from the same Latin root word. The key to genius is genuineness. The more you express who you truly are, the more your genius comes forth. By contrast, the more you sell out and try to be what you think you should be, or live up to others' expectations, the more you stifle your brilliance. Most great scientists, inventors, musicians, and artists are individualists, sometimes eccentric. They have the guts to be all of what they are, even if the package doesn't fit the mold. They let all their talents rip, and in so doing they contribute to the world in spectacular ways.

Here's to your genuine genius. I'll look for your book in the store.

For Reflection

1. As a child, did you adopt any limiting self-images? Do you remember an incident in which someone you respected defined you as less than whole and you accepted the idea? How did you go on to play out that belief?

2. How would you react if someone described you as a genius, a master, or enlightened? Is there any part of you that could identify with that description and accept it?

3. Is there someone in your life whom you now see as small? For a moment, visualize him or her as great and focus on the qualities you appreciate. Practice holding this new vision, and watch that person and your relationship transform.

Beggars and Choosers

*M*y plane landed at the Miami airport just before the airport closed in the face of oncoming Hurricane Irene. I forged my way to my hotel, hunkered down, and watched in awe as gale-force winds humbled tall palm trees and massive sheets of rain pelted the huge picture windows. Suddenly the hotel lost electric power. I lit a candle, meditated, and savored the force of nature surging around me. I must say I found the experience exhilarating! I remember that evening as one of my most enjoyable hotel visits.

The next morning after the storm abated, hotel guests scrambled to rearrange their flight schedules. As I stood at the public phone in the lobby, I heard a fellow in the booth next to me talking to an airline reservations agent. "I realize that beggars can't be choosers," he pleaded, "but is there any chance you can get me on this flight?"

His words reverberated in my psyche: *Beggars can't be choosers*. It is true. If you think you are a beggar—undeserving of the good things in life, required to earn your right to be happy and suffer to get what you want—you are certainly not in a position of choice. But if you recognize that you are a cocreator with God, literally an

expression of a God who delights in experiencing joy through you, then begging becomes meaningless, utterly contradictory to who you are and the way you were born to live.

Every day you must decide if you are a beggar or a chooser, for you will act and create results according to the identity you assume. If you believe you must grovel, plead, or struggle to manifest your dreams, the road to success can seem overwhelming, even frightening. But if you realize that every decision before you is an invitation to remember who you are and what you want, the process of choosing becomes exciting, and the courage to claim your dreams follows naturally and easily.

To choose is to be empowered. Every time you say "yes" to one path and "no" to another, life rushes to support you in your decision. Often it does not matter so much what you choose, but that you *do* choose. As Will Rogers stated, "If you sit in the middle of the road, you will get hit by traffic from both directions."

Many declarations from the Bible echo this wisdom: "So, because you are lukewarm . . . I am about to spit you out of my mouth" (not the most romantic image, but effective); "let your 'yes' be a 'yes,' and your 'no' be a 'no'; all else is of evil" (meaning that when we live with half-heartedness or ambiguity, we forsake our power to act effectively); in *The Gospel According to Thomas,* we are told, "If you bring forth what is within you, it will heal you; if you do not bring forth what is within you, it will kill you." Pundits have described the process thus: "Throw your heart over the fence, and your body will follow." "Boldness has genius, power, and magic in it." And "99 percent commitment is hard; 100 percent commitment is easy."

One day when I was first getting into metaphysics, I spent a day in New York City with a group of spiritually oriented friends. After our outing, we were driving toward the George Washington Bridge and trying to decide if we wanted to see a movie or go home. "What do you guys want to do?" asked the driver. "I need to know which road to take."

"I am okay either way," one fellow announced. Another echoed, "I am not attached." Another reported, "I am easy." My response was, "I will go with the flow." At that point, the driver stepped on the brake and pulled the car onto the shoulder of the road. He abruptly turned toward the back seat and with an air of authority announced, "Okay, you New Age flakos, this is one of those times when everyone is just going to have to tell the truth about what you really want—or else we are going nowhere."

The rest of us looked at one another sheepishly. Then one fellow spoke, "I'd rather go home." "Yes, me too," said another. "I'm not really in the mood for a movie," I admitted. "Yeah, let's just keep going," the last fellow suggested.

"Thank you," the driver replied smugly. "Now we can go home." He stepped on the gas.

We all get to go home when we make strong choices. Thoreau advised: "Go confidently in the direction of your dreams. Live the life you have imagined." William James offered a powerful formula for following through on any important life choice: (1) be bold, (2) begin now, and (3) no exceptions.

If your new life is going to be anything, it will be what you make it. You will make it magnificent not by begging, but by choosing. The best way to predict the future is to create it.

For Reflection

1. How have you empowered yourself by making strong choices? How have you disempowered yourself by vacillating or not deciding?

2. Do you have a role model for bold decision making? What do you notice about this person's vitality and success?

3. Is there a decision before you now that you have been putting off? How does it feel not to decide? If you had to decide today, what would you choose? Notice how it feels to choose.

Signs When You Need Them

*W*hile driving home one day, I noticed that someone had posted some cardboard signs along the roadside, leading guests to a party on my street. I live out in the country where there are no city blocks, many curving roads, and irregular intersections.

Whoever put out the signs had placed them at the crucial intersections. At every important choice point, an arrow showed the way to turn. Between the signs, I drove for long stretches past numerous smaller intersections and saw no posters. Then, when I again reached a larger intersection, there was another clear marker.

It occurred to me that this is how Spirit gives us guidance—we get signs when we need them. Spiritual insight comes on a need-to-know basis. When you arrive at a critical choice point, information shows up to help you decide. If you are not getting a sign, you are probably not at a crucial intersection. That's the time to just keep going and enjoy the ride. Something more needs to happen before you get the next piece of information. When you are ready to know, you will. If you don't know, it is not time yet. In the meantime, just breathe, trust, and find the blessing where you are.

If you are seeking direction, pray for guidance. Then let the Universe deliver your answer in the right way, place, and time. If, upon completing your prayer, you do not hear a voice boom from heaven, shout your name, and bellow *"This is what you must do!"* don't freak out. Give the Great Spirit a chance to send your message when you most need it. It will come.

Guidance often arrives in uncanny and synchronistic ways. A man at a seminar told me he had been praying for direction. Then one afternoon as he walked out of a restaurant, the wind blew a piece of paper against his knees. He picked it up and discovered it was a flyer for my seminar that evening. He attended and subsequently his life changed.

Another friend decided he wanted to become independently wealthy and retire at a young age. He prayed for help with this project. The next morning when he went out to jog, he saw a book someone had left on top of a trash can: *Your Money or Your Life.* He took the book, read it, and found the wisdom he needed. Now he is well on his way to riches and early retirement.

If, out of anxiety, you act prematurely to force your answer, you will jam the signal of your incoming guidance and delay its arrival. In such a situation, your wisest move is to step back from fear-motivated activity and instead follow the voice of trust. One day I was waiting to board an airplane when the agent announced that the takeoff would be delayed two hours due to a mechanical problem. Since I had been waiting to find out if my request for a first-class upgrade had been approved, I headed toward the desk to inquire about it. In front of me, however, a large group of people had formed a long line. I realized that I could spend a considerable amount of those two hours just standing in line, with no guarantee I would get an upgrade. So I decided not to try to manipulate the situation and just to trust that somehow it would all work out.

I had a pass to the executive lounge, so I went there, took a nap, made a few phone calls, enjoyed some refreshments, and returned to the gate about fifteen minutes before the new takeoff time. As I approached the gate, I heard an announcement: "Mr. Cohen, please come to the desk." Without missing a step, I walked over to the desk, where the agent informed me that my upgrade had cleared. Then she gave me the ticket without collecting my payment coupons. I started to walk away, but then decided that in honesty I should give her the coupons. I returned to the desk and offered the agent the coupons. She responded, "The computer here says the upgrade has been paid for, and that's good enough for me." I stepped onto the plane with a chuckle. I now recognize the experience as a lesson in trust. When I did not try to force the result, it came to me in a gentle and generous way.

I use a very successful method to receive guidance. I call it "The Truth Smoke-Out." Whenever I am not sure what to do, I say to the Universe: "Just show me what I am to do. I am willing to do whatever is in the best interest of everyone involved. Give me a clue, and I will follow." Then I release the situation. I give up any preconceived notion about how this is supposed to turn out and

when I am supposed to know. Sometimes the answer comes instantly, and sometimes it takes awhile. But it always comes.

In the Greek version of the Bible, the first translation from the original Aramaic, two different words are used for our word *time.* One is *chronos,* which is equivalent to our understanding of time in seconds, minutes, and hours. The other word is *kairos,* which can best be translated as "in God's time" or "at the right time" or "when the time is ripe." In our culture, we are used to living in *chronos.* But there is an entirely more meaningful element of time, which is *timing.* That's *kairos.* Practice living in *kairos,* and answers arrive at the perfect time. God is at least as smart as the person who put the signs up for the party.

For Reflection

1. Is there anything you want to happen but feel impatient because it hasn't happened yet? Can you see some way that things are unfolding in perfect timing?

2. What is your personal method of asking for and receiving guidance? How do you know it when it comes?

3. Do you feel ready to receive the guidance, manifestation, or answer to the prayer for which you have been asking?

You Can't Compete With Love

*A*t a seminar I presented in Greece, a woman named Georgia told that she had been married to a man who was emotionally absent. After long and frustrating attempts to infuse life into her marriage, Georgia felt she needed to leave. "I told my husband I wanted a divorce, but he refused to give it to me," she recounted. "So I decided that even if he didn't love me, *I* would love me. I decided to give myself the love and tenderness I had been seeking from him. So every day I wrote myself a long love letter telling myself how beautiful, wise, and desirable I am.

"Then one day my husband found one of these letters. Since it was unsigned, he assumed it was from another man. The next day he came to me, waving the letter in his hand. He told me, 'I can't compete with this—you can have your divorce!'"

Everyone and everything that shows up in our lives is a reflection of what is happening inside of us. All events and experiences in our field of awareness outpicture a feeling, belief, or attitude we are holding. Thus we can use every experience as a barometer of where we are on our path. As a famous poet noted, "We think in secret and it comes to pass; environment is our looking glass."

Looking In for Number One

The law of attraction implies that we "hire" everyone in our play of life to act out the script we have written. This is why many of us have experienced repetitious patterns of relationship, work, or health; the actors may be different, but their roles are the same. Eventually we recognize that it cannot be an accident that the same types of people show up doing the same things; it is *we* who have drawn them according to the signals we are sending out. As the spiritual teacher Emmanuel has said: "One is not invaded by darkness. One has courted that darkness. It is a matter of addressing the host rather than chastising the guests."

The good news about the law of attraction is that the moment we change our mind, heart, or attitude, the outer world must reflect it, often *immediately*. In Georgia's case, she was holding an unconscious attitude that she was unlovable and did not deserve a husband who was present and attentive. As soon as she grew beyond that limiting belief, Georgia released her husband as the cause of her emptiness. When she gave herself the love she sought, her husband had no choice but to match it or leave.

We can save ourselves a great deal of pain and escape the struggle of trying to endlessly manipulate the world to line up with our desires. The secret is to *determine what you would like to receive from other people and then give it to yourself.* This crucial shift can be difficult in a world where we are bombarded daily with the implication that we are empty and needy, and everything we want and need is somewhere else. We are taught that the big "It" awaits out there in a romantic partner, a hit record, a slimmer body, a new car, a more prestigious job, or a bigger house. The funny thing about getting things from out there is that if you did not know you were whole before you got the thing, you will not become whole when you get it; in fact, you will feel even more empty and confused. As Buddha asked, "If you do not get it from yourself, where will you go for it?"

Cool Runnings is a delightful movie (based on a true story) about a group of young Jamaican men who decide to enter the bobsled competition in the winter Olympics. The team faces and overcomes tremendous obstacles to make it to the competition. The night before the big race, one of the team members confides in the coach that if he returns home without a medal, he will feel like a failure. In response, the coach offers this young man some good advice: "If you're not enough without the medal, you'll never be enough *with* it."

We all want to be in love, and rightfully so. Love is our natural state, literally who we are. The question is not "Should we love?" but "Where will we find the love we desire?" If we designate another person as the source of our love, we set ourselves up for a roller-coaster ride. You may recognize the pattern: heady ecstasy followed by frustration and conflict. Sometimes our partners do things that make us feel loved, and sometimes they do things that make us feel unloved. In such a case, we have given our power away in a way most unkind (to ourselves), and we become little more than a yo-yo on the string of life.

There is another way to love, one far more rewarding. This way finds the source of our love, power, and life *within* us. This way teaches that our purpose is not to import love, but to express it. Instead of being a love seeker, we become a love finder. We do not wait for love; we *generate* it. Then we are free to bask in the warmth of our own beauty. We have found love within us, where it has been all the time and ever shall be.

> Those who go searching for love only find their
> own lovelessness.
> But the loveless never find love; only the loving find
> love,
> And they never have to search for it.
> —D. H. Lawrence

For Reflection

1. Are you in a relationship in which you feel unloved? What do you think would happen if you gave yourself the love you are seeking from the other person?

2. Why do you think they call it a "crush"?

3. Do you experience any repetitive patterns in your relationships? What have you "hired" the other actors in your play to help you learn?

Never the Same Trip

I chuckled as I stepped from the rental car pavilion onto the shuttle bus to the Kauai airport. The road to the terminal was quite short, forming a circle of about a quarter mile; if I had walked the straight shot rather than taking the bus, I probably would have gotten there quicker!

I set my bags on the rack, took a seat, and nodded to the driver. He closed the door and stepped lightly on the gas. I joked, "I'll bet you get pretty bored making the same trip in circles all day!"

The fellow turned his head slightly, smiled politely, and answered, "I've never made the same trip twice."

Oh.

"I always meet interesting people on the bus," he added. "I like to talk to them and find out where they're from. They usually have some good stories about their vacations. I love this job!"

Oh.

What a huge lesson this humble driver taught me! I was stuck in circular thinking. He was glowing with joy. He took a potentially monotonous job and transformed it into a game he just kept winning. As the ecstatic Persian poet Hafiz declared, "It's all just a big love contest, and I never lose."

101

Boredom is not a condition; it is an attitude. Anything can be boring if you bring a closed mind to it. Anything can be fascinating if you bring an open mind to it. You can make anything out of anything.

A woman once sent me a small stone with a pencil drawing on it. The rendering clearly depicted the profile of a woman looking up at a bird. It was quite beautiful. As I looked more closely at the stone, I saw that the artist had not etched these lines; she simply traced some lines that were already in the stone. As I read the enclosed letter describing her art business, I learned that she takes objects from nature and finds patterns in them. Then she highlights those patterns. She does not consider herself a creator; she is a magnifier. Her art reminded me of Michelangelo's famous response when he was asked how he crafted a sculpture as magnificent as *David.* "I just saw David in the stone," he explained, "and then I chipped away everything that was not David."

I am amazed as I observe little children watch the same video over and over and over again. My goddaughter watched *Three Men and a Baby* twenty-one times! An adult would be bored after the second or third viewing. But children have a wonderful ability to always find something novel and fascinating. They do not undermine new experiences by trying to stuff them into old boxes. They live in the thrilling now moment, which is always fresh and alive. As the mystic Kabir noted, "Wherever you are is the entry point."

The closest experience I can equate to watching videos repeatedly is listening to inspirational cassette tapes. I have listened to some of the same tapes many times, and I do not get bored. To the contrary, I hear new material every time. On one of my favorite tapes, a workshop participant asked Abraham how it feels to keep answering the same questions over and over again. "Oh, we've never answered the same question twice!" Abraham responded. I wonder if Abraham knows the shuttle bus driver.

My young friend Matthew, whom you met in an earlier chapter, keeps me on my toes. One day when I went to visit his family, he greeted me at the door and asked, "How are you, Alan?"

"Just fine, Matthew," I told him.

Ten minutes later he asked again, "How are you, Alan?"

My first impulse was to tell him, "You just asked me that, and I told you I'm fine." But just as I was about to speak, I stopped and realized this was another Matthew moment. Ten whole minutes had elapsed since our last conversation. All kinds of things could have happened in those ten minutes! In that period of time, people are born, people die, people have orgasms, people get enlightened, and in the ocean just a few miles down the road, billions of undersea creatures go through zillions of microscopic life cycles. For some critters, ten minutes is the span of their whole life. If I were fully open and available to the flow of Spirit, I could be an entirely different person in ten minutes! Of course, Matthew had every right and reason to ask me such an illuminated question.

Scientists tell us that there is no cell in our bodies more than seven years old. Every organ is constantly rebuilding itself with new cells. Why, then, does your body look the same, or older? Because the new cells go into old patterns that are perpetuated by repetitious thinking.

If you could think and feel anew with every new moment, you would hardly age. In fact, if anyone asks you how old you are and you answer with any number over seven years, you are fibbing.

I think that Matthew, the Kauai shuttle bus driver, Abraham, all the children of the world, and all the animals are in cahoots. I think they get together and have secret meetings to figure out how to surprise, confound, and entertain the rest of us who are marooned in the past and future. They are dispatched by an insidiously brilliant conspiracy designed to keep us from getting hung up in our creaking beliefs. Thank God for innocent souls who delight in life; otherwise, we might have it all figured out, and then what would we do?

In the Bible, when Moses approaches the burning bush on Mt. Sinai, God tells him, "Take off your shoes, for you are standing on holy ground." The same instruction applies to us: Wherever you stand is holy ground. Wherever there is life, the ground is holy. Life is everywhere; the question is, are you in it?

No, it's never the same trip. God is too original to do the same thing twice.

For Reflection

1. Are you involved in any activities you find boring? Is there another way you could look at them so they become more alive?

2. The next time you see your spouse, best friend, or employer, imagine you are meeting that person for the first time, without any history or preconceived ideas about who he or she is.

3. Put this book aside for a moment and look around at your surroundings. What beauty, art, or inspiration can you find that you had not noticed before?

Reality Check

*I*spent some time with John Perkins, author of the fascinating book *Spirit of the Shuar.* John's amazing story began in the 1960s, when he joined the Peace Corps to avoid the draft. John was assigned to live with the Shuar tribe in Ecuador. His mission: to educate the Shuar how to build their financial investment portfolios. Now, this was a particularly challenging assignment, since the Shuar had no money, few possessions, and very little contact with the civilized world. In fact, the Shuar are the original headhunters (literally)— they invented the practice of shrinking heads. To this day, a young Shuar man passes his initiation to manhood by killing an enemy and bringing back his shrunken head. (And you thought your teenager's navel piercing was bizarre!)

John learned a little Spanish and set up a series of investment seminars for the Shuar. To his surprise, the classes were packed to overflowing, with hushed listeners hanging on every word. (Later John found out that his audience didn't understand a word he was saying—they were there just for the entertainment value of watching a crazy gringo guy go on about nothing.)

After a short time in the jungle, John became severely ill, and a Shuar shaman was called to heal him. The healing, John recounts, was extraordinary, and he became a convert to the Shuar way of life. John went on to live with the tribe for many years, justifying his continued presence to his draft board by sending them an annual letter convincing them he was saving the world from communism.

Over time, John became fascinated with the sexual mores of the Shuar, which are quite sophisticated. Like many indigenous peoples, the Shuar have a healthful, playful attitude toward sex. And, like the practitioners of Tantrism and the Kama Sutra, they have honed their practice of sexuality to a cultured art. For example (until missionaries convinced them otherwise), the Shuar would make love only in nature; they felt that being in the great outdoors increased their sense of oneness with nature and their partner. (I think they're on to something there!)

Furthermore, an older Shuar man customarily takes a younger woman as his wife and teaches her the secrets of lovemaking. Then, after he grows older and dies, she takes a younger husband and trains him in the ancient art. So the tradition goes on from generation to generation, assuring the continuity of quality lovemaking as taught by experienced elders.

One day several Shuar tribespeople asked John, "How do people in your culture learn about lovemaking?"

"Well," he answered hesitantly, "a couple of fifteen-year-old kids sneak out of the house, find the backseat of a car, and sort of figure it out."

"My God," the elders exclaimed, aghast. "How primitive!"

While you and I have been led to believe that our version of reality is the only one or the wisest one, there are many other perspectives that can enrich us. What we call

"reality" is but one tiny aspect of the "big picture." If we can open our minds to peer through another lens, we can discover ways of living that can enhance our own.

I have learned a great deal by traveling throughout the world and meeting people of many different cultures. In Bali, I learned that happiness does not depend on having material goods; joy is an inside job. In Russia, I discovered that the human spirit cannot be dampened by political oppression. In Mexico, I saw how life revolves around families who love and care about one another above all else. In Greece, I discovered that passion can be a way of life. And on, and on. We can learn something valuable from every culture, and it from us. Like the five blind men groping to define an elephant, we each have a piece of reality that makes sense only when we contribute our perspective and are open to accept other perspectives, as well.

Ram Dass tells of a time when, during his drug experimentation days, he found himself backstage at the Newport Jazz Festival. While under the influence of a hallucinogen, he saw a peephole in the back of the tent and, just for fun, he looked out of it. To his surprise, he saw another eye looking back at him. The two eyes stared into each other for a long time, quite fascinated with each other. Finally, Ram Dass heard a voice from the other side of the tent, obviously associated with the mysterious eye. The voice asked, "Wanna get in?"

The cosmic joke is that Ram Dass thought he was on the inside. Meanwhile, so did the other fellow. Who was truly on the inside? Both of them. Each was on the inside of his own reality, as we all are.

What seems quite sophisticated to us may be primitive to others, and that which we judge to be Neanderthal may offer more value than we recognize. Wisdom has a way of showing up in the strangest places. Wanna get in?

For Reflection

1. Have you ever experienced a shift in consciousness that showed you there was more to reality than the reality you had known? What did you learn?

2. Explain in your own words the meaning of the question, "Would you rather be right or happy?"

3. What do you believe indigenous people have to offer the modern world?

Who's Sorry Now?

*A*t a spiritual retreat, a group of participants and I sat in a Native American sweat lodge. We huddled together, perspiring copiously in the dark hut, with hot steam dripping on our backs and tingling our noses. The leader began the ceremony with a series of chants and prayers. At one point, he entered into a prayer of apology: "Oh, Great Spirit," he called out loudly, "I'm sorry for not being a better leader, for not making the fire hot enough, and for not respecting You." He went on to enumerate a lengthy list of his other sins. Then he turned to the group and asked, "Is anyone else here sorry for anything?" Then he waited for more sins to be confessed. And he waited. And he waited.

Finally, one woman called out from the darkness, "We're not that kind of group." Immediately the group broke into welcome laughter. We were not that kind of group. We had spent an intensive week (and many years) reclaiming our innocence, and the idea of guiltily begging God for forgiveness seemed quite the non sequitur.

Many of us grew up under the influence of the notion that we are all basically evil, bearing the awful burden of original sin that made us guilty just for being born. This means there was something wrong with you before you even had a chance to do something wrong! Such a notion is quite counterproductive to a healthful spiritual psyche. It keeps us small, needy, owing, and controllable by those who profess our guilt. If you buy it, you get to live with it.

There is, of course, another way to look at ourselves. This vision sees us as pure children of God, created, as the Bible says, in God's image and likeness. We have never done anything that could cause us to be separate from God, and we certainly are not guilty for the sins of those who came before us. We are whole, wise, and divine, sojourning through an adventure on Earth to rediscover the wonder of the Spirit within us. Yes, we make mistakes. No, we are not evil.

I used to live much of my life apologetically. Somewhere in my mind I labored under the notion that I was a mistake, bothering the world simply by being here. Everyone else had a right to their good, but if anything good happened to me, I was just lucky. I feared that if people found out who I really was, I would be exposed and shunned.

Funny thing is, now that I have worked with thousands of people in individual and group counseling situations, nearly all of them believed there was something wrong with them. I have seen the most attractive and successful people display the lowest self-esteem. Out of the spotlight, they admit that their anxious striving for success was motivated by a need to prove themselves. (A magazine reporter asked Hollywood's top CEOs "What is your biggest fear?" Nearly all of them answered, "That people will discover I don't really know what I am doing.") If you do not recognize your intrinsic worth, all the accolades you collect will not fill the illusory black hole, but only darken it.

The more you try to protect, defend, prove, or explain yourself, the farther you drift from authentic confidence. If someone does not want to accept you, no sales job is sufficient, and if someone accepts you, no sales job is necessary. Likewise, if someone wants to keep you guilty, no apology is acceptable, and if someone is willing to love you, no apology is necessary.

I know of two friends who wanted to break their habit of apologetic living, so they made a pact. When one said, "I'm sorry," the other replied, "You're not sorry—you're pathetic!" As you can imagine, they broke the habit quickly!

Does unapologetic living mean you are never supposed to say you're sorry? No, it means you dump the *attitude* of self-diminution. If you make a mistake and inadvertently hurt someone, certainly you might offer a sincere apology; you let him or her know you care and you would not repeat the same error. But then you get on with the joy of loving the person and yourself and celebrating the next moment.

A Zen story tells of two monks who were walking through a forest when they encountered a woman standing at the bank of a stream. She was anxious and afraid to ford the rushing waters. So one of the monks lifted the lady and carried her across the stream. The two monks continued on their way, but the second monk silently fumed for an hour. Finally, he blurted out, "You know it is against the rules of our order to touch a woman!" The other monk calmly answered: "Yes, but I put her down an hour ago. You're still carrying her."

Guilt and apologetic living are aberrations of a sacred experience called *contrition*. Contrition is the liberating realization that you have been living out of harmony with your good or that of others. Such awareness is not a cause for self-recrimination, but rejoicing. When you discover your error, you become inspired to live a better way. Some of the greatest saints, teachers, and world-change agents have the darkest histories. Yet something happened along their paths that caused them to wake up one morning and resolve, "There must be a better way." Paramahansa Yogananda said, "A saint is simply a sinner who never gave up." Terry Cole-Whittaker titled one of her books *Every Saint Has a Past, Every Sinner Has a Future*.

The most powerful way to grow beyond apologetic living is to *find the blessing in everything, including your mistakes*. Adopt the attitude that there is nothing outside the plan for your good and even your biggest "sin" is an integral element of your homecoming. Your mantras are "Thank you for everything" and "Everything serves." Then your friends can say to you, "You're not sorry— you're passionate."

For Reflection

1. Is there anything you repeatedly apologize for? How do you think this affects your relationships and your ability to succeed?

2. Are you berating yourself for errors you made in the past? How have those experiences blessed and served you?

3. Have you ever noticed that when you try to explain or defend yourself, you end up feeling smaller? The next time you are tempted to explain, stop and watch what happens.

The Hero Next Door

I met a musician named Lenny who grew up in Harlem in the 1950s and played jazz at local nightclubs. "I jammed with my friends every night," he told me. "One of them was Charlie Parker—before he became famous." Lenny laughed and added: "Just think—I hung out with one of the jazz greats of all time. I had no idea the guy playing right next to me would one day become a legend."

Lenny got me thinking. Every great person, from Galileo to St. Francis to Martin Luther King Jr., grew up as a normal person and did normal things with normal people. Probably none of their buddies expected that their friends would one day change the course of life on the planet and retool the destiny of humanity.

What if someone close to you, maybe your best friend, turned out to be a hero to millions? "Oh, that couldn't happen to anyone I know," you might answer hastily. But perhaps the friends of young Louis Pasteur might have spoken equally hastily.

The seeds of greatness can sprout anywhere, through anyone—sometimes in the least likely situation. I met a hypnotherapist who was approached by a man seeking hypnotherapy for his seventeen-year-old son who was having trouble with his golf game. The hypnotherapist thought

this would not be a valuable use of her time, so she turned the man down. "I'm sorry, Mr. Woods," she told him, "I won't be able to see your son . . ."

In 1985 I was invited to participate in a citizen diplomacy mission to the Soviet Union. The organizer asked if I knew anyone else who would be appropriate to attend. I immediately thought of my friend Dr. Patch Adams. I invited Patch, and he was thrilled at the prospect of going, so I sponsored him. During the trip, Patch met actor Mike Farrell (of *M*A*S*H* fame), and the two became friends. Fourteen years later, Mike Farrell produced a major motion picture of Patch's life. Little did I know when I invited Patch to join the trip that I was participating in a linkup that would eventually affect millions of people, as well as raise considerable funds for Patch's free hospital (Gesundheit Institute) in West Virginia.

Many heroes next door do not attain fame, but they are heroes nevertheless. What is a hero, but someone who lives true to his or her ideals and inspires others to do the same? My friend Dan served on the police force for several years and then became disillusioned with his profession. So he opened up a small restaurant, which he now operates with his family. Dan takes care of all his customers with utter kindness and gentleness, always looking to see what more he can do. Even more important, he is at peace with himself. He always has a smile, and the food is always great. The best part of the food is the love that Dan and his family serve with their meals.

Some of the greatest heroes escape our notice because we are looking right past them. One of my favorite moments in the Easter story occurs when Mary Magdalene goes to visit Jesus' tomb after his crucifixion. At that point, Mary does not know that Jesus has been resurrected, and she expects to find him in the tomb. But he is not there. Instead, Jesus appears to Mary outside the tomb. Certainly not expecting to find Jesus along her way, Mary thinks he is the gardener. How surprised she is when she finds that the gardener is actually Jesus!

Maybe your gardener is a hero. Maybe the toll collector or veterinarian or dentist or the homeless man on the exit ramp of the freeway is a hero. Because we are often distracted by worldly appearances and judgments, you might be overlooking the hero next door.

Now here's the kicker: the hero next door could be *you.* Just as you may have overlooked someone else's magnificence, you may have overlooked your own. Perhaps that book you've been playing with in your mind, or that song or painting or labor-saving device, is not some random thought, but a divinely inspired vision. Every great invention, philosophy, or Ivy League university started with just one tiny seed thought. The difference between those who struggle through life and those who succeed and serve in huge ways is simply that some people believe in their ideas and others don't.

It is said that anyone can count the number of seeds in an apple, but only God can count the number of apples in a seed. There are actually an infinite number of apples in a seed, but the number that sprout is a result of cultivation. At this moment there are an infinite number of ideas and talents within you, ideas that can change your life and the lives of millions—who knows, maybe the whole planet.

A writer became frustrated after several publishers rejected his manuscript. Exasperated, he threw the book into the wastebasket and gave up on the project. He was also a minister, and he figured he would just stick with what he was already doing.

The writer's wife, however, believed in him and his project. That night she retrieved the manuscript from the trash and encouraged him to submit it again. He decided to go along with her advice, and this time the book was accepted.

The writer was Dr. Norman Vincent Peale and the book was *The Power of Positive Thinking*, a now-classic inspirational text that has sold many millions of copies and changed the lives of vast numbers of readers.

Mrs. Peale had a notion that she might be living close to the hero next door. Maybe so do you. Maybe so does your neighbor.

For Reflection

1. Do you know anyone who has become famous or very successful? Did you think, at the time you knew the person, he or she would attain such fame?

2. What did Jesus mean when he said, "A prophet is never accepted in his own hometown"?

3. Are you open to the possibility that you could make a contribution to the world that would affect many lives and even alter the course of life on Earth?

Passion and Prayer

*T*he inspiring movie *Dangerous Beauty* recounts the story of Veronica, a sixteenth-century Venetian courtesan (noble prostitute) who wins the hearts of her clients. Veronica is beautiful, witty, and full of passion for life and her profession. Her clients sense her terrific life force, and they are lifted beyond the grayness of their lives.

The Inquisition overtakes Venice, and Veronica is brought to trial on charges of witchcraft. The judge sternly informs her that if she confesses to being a witch, her life will be spared. In a stirring courtroom soliloquy, Veronica declares: "I confess . . . I confess that I find more ecstasy in passion than in prayer. Such passion *is* prayer."

For those of us who have been taught that prayer or spirituality requires denying our passion, Veronica's statement may come as a shock. But, as Philip Brooks noted, "Prayer is not the overcoming of God's reluctance, but the taking hold of God's willingness." And what is God's willingness but the experience of joy and full aliveness in every arena of life?

While giving a talk at a church in a conservative region, I noticed that nearly everyone in the church looked the same. The women had the same hairdos, the men wore the same suits, and most of the conversations fell within a thin slice of the middle of the bell curve of the socially acceptable. If you saw the movie *Pleasantville,* you get the picture. There didn't seem to be much color, life, or expression of individual creativity in that group.

Just then, a teenage fellow with orange hair walked into the church. Now I confess that I have had judgments about people who dye their hair weird colors and have metal objects inserted in various bodily orifices. But that day I was really glad to see that guy. He was the only person in that church, as far as I could tell, who was making a statement for individual expression.

At another time I sat through a fairly subdued Christmas church service. As soon as the service was over and the attendees were milling out, some upbeat music came over the loudspeaker. I looked up into the balcony and saw two teenagers who came alive and started dancing to this music. Suddenly my heart lifted. It was the strongest expression of aliveness I had felt during the service. I think Jesus would have appreciated it too.

Then there was the time I spoke at a small church in the Midwest. That day the Sunday school teacher didn't show up, so the church elders took the class, which consisted of a half-dozen boys about the age of ten, and stuck them in the first row of the sanctuary, hoping this would keep the kids in line. My talk was about making the most of wherever you are. You can imagine my surprise when I looked over to see all the boys sitting there with quarters in their eye sockets! At first I was jarred, but then I had to hand it to them. They were the only people in the church who put my lesson into practice immediately!

A fun way to check in on your passion is by doing an energy scan on yourself or others. Have you ever seen a magazine or television advertisement for home insulation that shows a thermograph of a house in the wintertime? The photo shows most of the home as blue, indicating the areas that are well insulated. Some of the areas, especially around the doors and windows, glow red, pointing out the places where heat is leaking out.

Many of us have been trained to believe that life is about staying insulated, rather than glowing with passion. God, however, is most present and obvious where people are happy and alive. This means that there is more genuine prayer happening at football games than in many churches. If churches could work up enthusiasm, presence of attention, and spirit as well as professional football, religion in our country would really rock. But many people walk out of some churches more dead than alive. If we made a rule that next Sunday only those people who really love to go to church would go, I wonder what attendance would look like. The good news is that the energy in church would be spectacular. As a teacher or minister, I would rather teach to a small group who really wants to be there, than to a large group whose mind is on the golf course. To that group, I would say: "Please, go golf. Let the golf course be your church." Such passion *is* prayer.

Where there is passion, there is church. Where there is enthusiasm, there is God. True prayer is not mumbling a set of words, but energetically expressing what makes you feel most alive. When you love what you are doing, you become God in action.

For Reflection

1. What were you taught about prayer in the religion in which you were raised? Did you find this notion of prayer inspiring and enlivening?

2. Do you have the confidence to create your own prayers, fueled by passion and inspiration, rather than reciting rote words scripted by another?

3. Can you accept your passion as an expression of God in action?

Honey, Do

I have learned a lot about relationships from my friends who have tried various schemes to get hitched. They have tried personal ads, video dating services, Internet Web sites, New Age affirmations, matchmakers, astrological analyses, tantric retreats, Wicca rituals, and secret pheromone potions. One friend stood on her porch each morning and read aloud the qualities of her ideal mate. Another bought a wedding dress, set a date, and announced her wedding to her friends. "Who is the groom?" they asked her. "I'll tell you when I meet him," she answered.

One of my friends is a professional dater. Over many years Marilyn, an interior designer in Los Angeles, has placed numerous personal ads in many magazines. She has gone out on at least one date with hundreds of guys. But she finds something wrong with all of them. One guy is too flashy, another too cheap; one man wants too much sex, another is celibate; one fellow talks too much, another is too quiet. She says she wants a mate, but I think she really just likes to date. That's fine; it's a choice. Dating can be a very illuminating spiritual path. It's just important to tell the truth about what you really want. You can always tell what you want by what you are getting.

By contrast, I know a man named John who lived as a

hermit in the remote Halawa Valley on the sleepy Hawaiian island of Molokai. To get to John's house, you would have to travel for several hours over a long and winding road, then park your car on the property of a backcountry family who (for $3) will protect your car (from themselves), and then hike into a secluded rainforest so far off the grid it makes Gilligan's Island look metropolitan. That jungle is inhabited by societal dropouts, pot growers, holed-up army vets still on the lookout for Viet Cong and, who knows, maybe bigfoot.

One day John's buddy Hank showed up for a visit along with Hank's friend Cheryl. Long story short, John and Cheryl fell in love, moved back to civilization, got married, had children, and enjoy a lovely life together. No video dating, no personal ads, and no "I have a friend I'd like you to meet." Just the law of attraction. When you are ready to receive what you want, it will find you.

If you are not ready, your good may be seeking you, but you won't recognize it. A man at a seminar complained he was unable to meet the right woman. He desperately wanted his mate, but everyone he dated was a disappointment. The more he spoke during the seminar, the more striking was the contrast between his words and his attitude. His mouth was declaring, "I am ready for my lady!" yet his energy was screaming, "I can't have it!" He would talk for a minute about his desire, and for the next ten minutes grumble about what's wrong with women. His investment in his problem outweighed his investment in his solution. My guess is that if he really wants a lady, his excitement about having a partner will have to outgrow his determination to be right about what's wrong.

Adventures in Uncommon Sense

In one of my programs in California, a dear young lady, age sixteen, asked: "But what if my soulmate is in North Carolina? How will we find each other?" The audience giggled in the face of her innocence. The law of attraction is not bound by geography or social scheming. People who match each other will meet. When you are ripe for someone or something, you will draw it unto you.

There are a million ways you can meet the right person for romance, friendship, business, or spiritual growth. One of my friends met his wife when she picked him up hitch-hiking. I know one fellow who, while living with a group of bachelors, made a bet that he could get a date with one of the girls who lived in an apartment down the hall. He won the bet, picked one girl, and now they have been married for over thirty years.

Then there was Lorenzo, who got divorced, moved to Hawaii, and built a house there. One day Lorenzo received a phone call from a woman who had dialed a wrong number. When he asked her what number she was trying to reach, the number was so unlike his number (including a completely different area code) that the two tried to figure out how her call might have been directed to him. Finally, he asked her, "What kind of phone are you using?" When she described it, Lorenzo realized this was a phone he had once owned and sold to someone. His number was still imbedded in the speed-dial feature, and when the woman had placed her call, she "accidentally" activated the speed-dial sequence. The two got to talking and liked each other. A few months later Lorenzo flew to Utah to meet this woman. Three months later they were married.

Destiny? Perhaps. Intention? For sure. Both Lorenzo and

his mystery caller were open and ready for a relationship, and the Big Phone Company in the Sky arranged their meeting. Sound easy? It is. What's the catch? You have to do your inner work first. It doesn't just happen. It happens when you choose it.

Methods are just excuses to focus your attention while you build up energy to magnetize what you want. They are helpful if you use them rather than letting them use you. Dating and mating are a form of creating. Creation is seeded with vision, framed by belief, fueled by desire, and completed by acceptance. Lorenzo knows; right about now he's quite glad that he programmed his speed-dial.

For Reflection

1. Is destiny something that is set up before you arrive on Earth, or is it something you create as you go?

2. Have you ever wished for something that did not happen until you firmly chose it to happen?

3. How is the law of attraction operating in your relationship(s) now? If you can tell what you want by what you get, what is the mirror of your life reflecting to you?

Date With Destiny

A cynical man came to the rascal sage Nasrudin and challenged him, "If you can show me where God is, I will give you an orange." Nasrudin thought for a moment and answered, "If you can show me where God is not, I will give you two oranges."

Do you believe that God is willing to meet and guide you right where you are, working wonders around you and *through* you?

At a weekend seminar I presented in Greece, an amiable gentleman named George invited me to lunch on the following day, and I accepted. When the time came, however, I felt as if an invisible hand was pressing against me, as if to say, "Do not go." My strongest desire at that moment was to return to my hotel room and rest. I felt a bit guilty about canceling my appointment, but I decided to go with my instinct. I told George that I needed some quiet time and suggested that we might sit together that evening at a nightclub gala for the seminar participants.

When I arrived at the nightclub, I saved George a seat next to me, but he never filled it. Later that evening I found George sitting in a distant booth with a lovely woman. When I told him I had saved him a seat, he laughed and explained that he had a date with destiny.

"This afternoon when we did not go to lunch together, I went out with some of the seminar participants," George explained. "There I met Helen and, as you can see, we really hit it off!" George and Helen smiled and toasted their champagne glasses to their meeting.

I smiled, too, as I made my way back to my seat, considering the powerful synchronicity that had occurred. It was absolutely perfect—nothing less than divine guidance—that I felt moved to cancel my lunch with George. Even while guilt tugged at me, I was assisting him to be in his right place to fulfill his heart's desire.

My encounter with George is not an isolated miracle. At every moment the voice of wisdom is emanating from within your soul, broadcasting impeccable guidance like a radio station always on the air. The voice of God is as loud as your willingness to listen.

When you find yourself at the crossroads of choice, practice moving with your joy instinct. Simply feel inside yourself and notice which alternative rings with the most aliveness. What would you really *like* to do? If, like many people, you attended school at "Our Lady of Perpetual Suffering," you may have been taught that you gain "God Brownie Points" by sacrificing your happiness and bearing the old rugged cross. But, as Dolly Parton suggested in the movie *Straight Talk,* "Get off the cross, honey— somebody needs the wood."

There are a lot better things that God has in store for you than pain. God does not crucify us; we crucify ourselves. The word *sacrifice* means "to make sacred." Suffering is not sacred, but joy is. Can you trust that God wants you to be happy and choose joy rather than self-punishment?

In preparation for one of my Mastery Training seminars in Hawaii, I spoke with a prospective participant named Judy who felt torn between using her few thousand dollars of savings for the seminar and trip or saving the money in her retirement fund. "I really want to be in the seminar, but I've never really spent money on things that are fun," Judy confessed. "I've always been very practical and penny-conscious. But my life is boring and my health is troubled."

As Judy spoke, I remembered a favorite quote: "If you always do what you've always done, you'll always get what you've always gotten." I suggested to Judy that if she was unhappy with the life she had created, saving money for more of the same life would not do her much good. I suggested that she invest in herself and make a space for joy in her life. Judy conceded that her money was not really helping her if she was using it to continue an unhappy pattern, and she courageously agreed to adventure to Hawaii.

At the Mastery Training, Judy skyrocketed in self-appreciation and experienced a profound transformation. On the evening of graduation, she announced that she had phoned the airline and requested an upgrade to first class for her flight home—to the tune of an additional $842! Judy had truly gotten the idea that life is about expansion and money is for celebration!

When I spoke to Judy a few weeks later, she told me that she had enjoyed first class so much that she stayed awake during the entire overnight flight—and she intended to find a way to fly first class from now on. More-over, when she arrived home she discovered that she had more funds available in the account she thought she had depleted! In fact, the money she discovered was equal to the amount she had invested.

The Bible tells us, "Choose ye this day whom you will serve." Faith or fear. Joy or pain. Celebration or apology. There is nothing blind about our date with destiny.

For Reflection

1. Is there anything you would like to do, but are not doing it because you might not live up to someone else's expectations? Is there any way that following your instinct might actually serve the other person?

2. Take a day to practice moving with your instincts. Let intuition guide all your decisions and act on the strongest energy you feel in any given moment. Note the results.

3. How might your gut feelings be connected to your destiny? How do you think God gets people to live their purpose?

Truth or Etiquette?

"I realized my friend was drunk when she began to weave recklessly in and out of the highway lanes," Rosemary told me. "Sitting in the passenger seat, I knew I had to take over the wheel of the car. *I didn't want to hurt her feelings, but I knew we were going to die."*

A classic quote, to be sure. You and I have experienced variations on the theme: "I am dying in my relationship, but I feel too guilty to leave." "I hate my job, but I don't know how the company will get along without me." "My best friend is working himself to death, but he gets mad when I confront him."

Ram Dass's guru tested him by asking, "Does truth come from good, or does good come from truth?" Good, Ram Dass discovered, comes from truth. If you are busy trying to do the expected thing, look cool, or protect someone from being hurt (including yourself), you will probably have to go back and speak the truth you were inclined to tell at first. It is important to be good, but it is more important to be real.

The kindest gift you can offer a friend is the truth. If you hold love in your heart and sincerely seek to serve, you can deliver any message in a helpful way. The words

are not as important as your purpose; the most important element of effective communication is caring.

My friend Lani owns a bookstore that is a popular refuge for spiritual seekers. Many regular customers and passersby find solace when they visit the peaceful shop. The staff is always friendly and helpful, and they often serve as counselors and nurturers.

When Lani told me she had hired a certain local businesswoman to take over as manager, I felt my solar plexus contract. The woman she chose was an abrasive "in-your-face" salesperson with a reputation for alienating her clients. With some trepidation, I told Lani of my reservations about her choice. Lani reacted defensively, asserting that she had made up her mind. I reasoned that I had delivered my suggestion, and I let the situation go.

Several months later Lani called to tell me she had fired the manager; the woman had turned off customers, and the store was losing business. In the aftermath, Lani thanked me for my honesty. "At first, I thought you were against me, and I got angry. Now I realize you were trying to help me, and I appreciate our friendship even more."

Would you like more intimacy in your relationships? The word *intimacy* can be broken down into three words that hint at the key to attaining it: *into me see*. When you let others see who you really are, you develop trustworthy relationships based on integrity. Why would you stay in a relationship or a job that you have to lie to keep? If you trust that who you are is good enough and that your path is divinely guided, then the Universe will match you with people and situations aligned with you and your purpose.

If a job, relationship, or friendship is not working for

you, it can't really be working for the other person. The only way anyone wins is when everyone wins. If you voice your concerns about a relationship or job and receive the response, "Things are great—what's your problem?" you have probably hit a wall of denial. A more affirmative response would be: *Let's talk about what we can do so we all feel taken care of.*

Here are a few guidelines for delivering the truth in a way that will work for both you and the recipient.

1. **Speak gently.** You don't have to yell or attack to get your point across. A few clear words, stated firmly, from the heart, will move mountains.

2. **Act promptly.** Speak your truth as soon as you know it. The longer you wait, the more confused and frustrated you will feel, the more resentment you will amass, and the more difficult it will be to finally express it.

3. **Own it.** Make "I" statements. Talk about your own experience, rather than laying responsibility on others.

4. **Focus on the solution rather than the problem.** Once you've stated your concern, get on with discovering and enacting the solution. Faultfinding keeps you in the problem.

5. **Look for a win-win resolution.** There is a way it can work for everyone. Make your partner's well-being as important as your own. Keep scanning for solutions until you hit on one that everyone can accept.

6. **Don't stop until you feel complete.** Handle it all, so you can get on with your life.

7. ***Call upon help from a Higher Power.*** Invite Spirit into the situation to handle what you cannot.

Love sees beyond defenses and plumbs to the core of the heart. Someone who is hurting himself or herself is calling for support. Summoning integrity is more important than protecting an illusion that hurts everyone who participates in it. "I didn't want to hurt her feelings, but I knew we were going to die," calls for loving honesty. Take care of yourself, speak your truth, and everyone will live.

For Reflection

1. Is there anyone to whom you have put off expressing yourself because you are afraid? What would you say if you were not afraid? Can you think of a way to speak your truth that is loving and takes into account the listener's feelings as well as your own?

2. Are there any situations in which you feel resentful because you have not expressed yourself? Can you see how withholding self-expression builds animosity?

3. How could speaking your truth be a service to the recipient?

Ring Out the Old

*W*hen I saw an advertisement for a fantastic new cell phone deal that would upgrade my current service, I called the telephone company and placed an order. I was told that the response to the promotion was so great that there would be a thirty-to-ninety-day wait for the phone. Okay, I can wait, I thought; after practicing meditation for all these years, I have learned at least *a little* patience (maybe).

Eleven days later while I was driving into town, I dialed a call from my cell phone. To my surprise, I received the message: "Your phone is not authorized for use. Please call the business office." God bless the phone company, I thought.

When I called the business office, the representative told me she had no clue why my phone wouldn't access. My bill was paid, and their diagnostic test showed no problem. I talked to several more reps, none of whom had any answers. Try calling later, they told me. God bless the phone company.

When I arrived home later that day, I found a FedEx box on my doorstep. Inside was my new cell phone. I plugged it in, and *voila!* it worked like a charm. The phone

company had disconnected my old phone because it had transferred service to my new one.

There's a lesson here: If the old thing isn't working anymore, it will do you no good to fight to reinstate it or keep it alive. Instead, focus your attention on the new thing, and what you need will appear at the right time, in the right way.

Timing and readiness are intrinsic elements of spiritual mastery. If you try to hang on to something that has outlived its usefulness, you will create stress, confusion, and counterproductive results. You will feel as if you are in limbo, flying midair between trapezes with no safety net. At such a point, your strongest strategy is to admit there is no going back and marshal all your energy in a forward direction. If there is nothing more you can do this moment, simply wait and hold the vision.

If your efforts to make something happen are not working, you may not be complete with the old thing. If you want a new relationship, but you are still attached or in love with a past partner, it's going to be tricky for a new partner to work his or her way through your blocked force field. If you want a new car, but you are sentimentally attached to your old falling-apart vehicle, you obstruct your own path. If you want to find a good employee, but you harbor a belief that "good help is hard to find," good help *will* be hard to find—not because this is a universal Truth, but because your thought makes it so.

Stop and ask yourself: "Am I ripe and ready to receive my goal? Do I have any internal conflict about this happening? Is there something about the old situation I am holding on to? Do I have any doubts or fears about moving ahead? Am I driving with one foot on the gas and the other on the brake?" If you can get in touch with any mixed intentions, you will bring them to light and be one step closer to resolving them.

And how do you let go of your old boyfriend, car, or beliefs? You sit down with yourself and get really honest. You conduct a fearless and searching self-inventory. You ask yourself if it is possible or realistic to re-create your past relationship; if driving an undependable car is truly serving you; or if you would rather be right about the scarcity of good help, than find someone who would do an effective job. Stimulate your sense of how good it would feel to have a joyful relationship with someone who is fully present, a car that gets you where you want to go when you want to get there, or a business that hums because your employees show up and do their jobs with skill and enthusiasm. When your excitement about having what you want outweighs your investment in what you don't want, you are in a perfect position to receive it.

When you line up your energy with your dream instead of your problem, you will receive signs and help from the Universe. Sometimes the old situation gets worse, underscoring the contrast that has motivated you to seek the new thing. Suddenly your decision becomes clear, and moving ahead becomes your only option.

During the first evening of a two-day seminar I conducted, a fellow stood up and made a profound profession of love to his girlfriend. "I admit that I have been holding out on our relationship and keeping my heart protected," Josh confessed. "Now I want to go deeper. I love you more than I have ever let you know, and I want to create a magnificent relationship with you." By the time Josh completed his poetic offering, there was not a dry eye in the room. Everyone was touched by his eloquent sincerity.

The next evening Josh showed up at the program alone. "Where is your girlfriend tonight?" I asked him. "She broke up with me today," Josh answered.

I was not surprised. Josh and his girlfriend had been operating at a relatively shallow level of intimacy. When Josh declared his intention to move deeper, he offered his partner a bold invitation to go deeper with him. But she was not ready. More intimacy was frightening to her. So she left. She could, of course, have chosen to join him on the journey, but she was not ready. I told Josh not to worry, for he had established a new depth of willingness in his relationships. Either his girlfriend would grow to meet him there, or he would meet someone else who matched his new intention.

When your intention is clear, the Universe will assist you to manifest it. You don't have to fuss about the old thing that is broken; you just have to be totally committed to the new thing that works. Then, when you least expect it, you will come home and find a colorful package at your door.

For Reflection

1. Is there something you have been doing for a long time that you would like to be done with? What would you rather be doing? Make a list of why you want something more satisfying and why you deserve it.

2. If you are seeking a goal that has not shown up yet, how does this situation match your inner intentions? Is there a part of you that is holding on to the old or resisting the new?

3. Describe in your own words the meaning of the affirmation: *God's timing is perfect.*

Where the Answer Lives

An ancient myth tells that when human beings were about to be created, a committee of gods got together to decide where the secret of life should be hidden. All the gods were in agreement that the secret should be concealed somewhere clever, so people would have an adventure to find it. But the gods had a hard time agreeing where it would be most challenging for people to locate the treasure.

"Let's hide the secret of life at the top of the highest mountain!" one god suggested.

"No, no," replied another. "People will invent airplanes and helicopters and rappelling equipment, and then everyone will be able to get to it."

"Then how about at the bottom of the sea?" another god posed.

"Same thing," another deity responded. "They will invent diving equipment and submarines, and that will be the end of the game."

The gods sat around, hands on chins, nearly stumped, until one god lit up. "I have it!" he exclaimed. "Let's hide the answer within each person—they'll *never* think to look there!"

And so it has turned out. When we need to know a truth,

we tend to look outside ourselves for answers, and the last place we look is in our own hearts. Meanwhile, all that we could ever need to know abides at the core of our being.

The great inventor Thomas Edison used this principle when he needed help with an invention. When Edison felt stymied in the midst of a difficult experiment, he would lie down on a couch with a rock in his hand. As he dozed off into a light sleep, he sank into his subconscious mind, which he recognized to be the avenue of infinite intelligence from which his best ideas sprang. Then, as his body relaxed, Edison would let loose of his hold on the rock, which would drop to the floor with a loud thud that would startle him out of his nap. At that moment Edison still had fresh in mind the idea he had contacted in his sleep state, and he would quickly write it down. That was Edison's secret. He went on to generate 1093 patents including the electric light, the phonograph, the alkaline battery, and motion pictures.

When I studied organizational development in graduate school, my professor wrote a sentence on the blackboard that ultimately meant more to me than all the techniques I learned. It said: "A consultant is someone who borrows your watch to tell you what time it is."

The greatest service any therapist, teacher, psychic, astrologer, or counselor can offer you is to remind you of what you already know. You have probably sought help or advice from several people or resources and still felt unfulfilled. Then someone said something that really resonated within you, and you said, "That's it!" How did you know *that* was it? Why did that one piece of advice move you more than the others? You already knew, and you were just waiting for someone to call your attention to the answer that matched your inner knowing.

Norman Vincent Peale was sitting on an airplane next to a young woman who struck up a conversation with him. When she discovered that Dr. Peale was a man of seasoned wisdom, she decided to ask him for help with a dilemma. "I have been dating two men and both of them have proposed to me," she explained. "I'm not sure which one to say 'yes' to. Can you give me some advice?"

"Sure," Dr. Peale answered abruptly in his famous gravelly voice. "I don't think you should marry either of them."

"Why is that?" asked the young lady, surprised.

"If you have to ask me whom to marry, you're not in love with either of them," he answered.

When something is really right for you, you know it. And when something is not right for you, you know it. Your job is not to find someone else to dictate your truth, but to get in touch with your inner knowing. Trust your intuition and gut feelings. Your inner wisdom is always speaking to you. Honor what your heart is telling you, and you befriend an impeccable guide that will take you all the way home.

For Reflection

1. Do you tend to value other people's advice more than your own intuition?

2. Think of the teacher, minister, counselor, therapist, author, or guru whom you most respect. What is it about this person you most appreciate? Do you believe this person respects you?

3. Have you had any dreams or hints of guidance recently that are giving you a clue to the answer you've been seeking?

The Five Golden Doors

*P*rosperity is far more than a healthy bank account—it is an attitude, a way of life that expresses itself in everything you do. When you latch onto the principle that there is enough of everything for everyone and that you can have all that your heart desires, your world expands immeasurably and you gain access to the riches of the universe.

The journey to prosperity is like a walk through a great mansion. Visualize a series of five adjoining rooms, each with a golden door leading to the next. To arrive at your goal you must master the lesson of each room. Then, when you have walked through the five doors, you are home.

Below are the keys to each of the five golden doors. Turn them by practicing the principles, and you will claim dominion over real and abiding wealth.

DOOR 1: YOU WILL MANIFEST AS MUCH AS YOU BELIEVE IS AVAILABLE.

Prosperous people understand that we live in an affluent universe capable of supplying all our needs. When Ted Turner donated one billion dollars to the United Nations, he declared, "The world is awash with money." Mr. Turner did not say so because he has a lot of money; he has a lot of money because he believes it. And it is so.

Utter enoughness is an eternal universal condition. A sense of lack is a trick of the mind, which is powerful enough to create shortage by its belief in it. A number of years ago a *tsunami* (tidal wave) warning was issued where I live. Many of the local residents rushed to the grocery stores and bought all the rice off the shelves. If you showed up at the end of the day, there was a rice short-age. Yet the shortage was created by fear; if customers took just what they needed, there would have been enough for everyone. Fortunately, the tidal wave never happened, yet it took several weeks for the stores to replenish their supplies. God did not create the shortage; people created it out of fear of not enough.

When faced with apparent lack, ask yourself, "Is this the truth or is it a temporary appearance? Is this shortage a natural condition or is it the result of limited thinking?"

Then turn your attention to abundance. Behold the sweeping expansive sky, the vast fathomless ocean, the stately mountains, and the infinite teeming life forms that populate this planet. Consider all the fields growing crops around the world and all the people being fed. Then look up into the staggering night sky and behold millions of stars in millions of galaxies. The universe is created in abundance of all things, and we have access to it all. "It is the Father's good pleasure to give you the kingdom." Proceed as if you have enough, and you will.

DOOR 2: YOU WILL MANIFEST AS MUCH AS YOU BELIEVE YOU DESERVE.

Your power to manifest is directly linked to your self-image. If you believe you are unworthy, sinful, or owe a karmic debt, your good will stop at that point—not because God withholds riches from you, but because you are withholding love from yourself. If you recognize yourself to be whole, loveable, and an heir to all that God has created, you accept your spiritual inheritance and you will walk in Heaven even while on Earth.

People with money don't doubt themselves. They value money and its place in their lives. They do not apologize for their wealth, and they spend it on things they enjoy. They know they deserve it; if they didn't, it would not stay long with them. Money comes to you, stays with you, and leaves you by right of your consciousness. You will magnetize prosperity in accord with your sense of worthiness. Know your immeasurable worth, and you will be immeasurably rich.

DOOR 3: YOU WILL MANIFEST AS MUCH AS YOU ASK FOR.

Many people ask or pray not for what they want, but what they think they can get. The lower your expectations, the smaller your results. The asking stage of manifestation is a crucial one. At that point you set a benchmark for everything that happens after that. Asking is like going out into a field and setting the markers for a house you intend to build. Be sure it is the size you want, for once the building begins, it will be difficult to change the dimensions.

Whenever you negotiate for a salary, sell a car or home, visualize to attract a mate, set a weight goal, or pray for any result, ask for all of what you want. You will be surprised to find that the Universe matches your request.

Your asking is in direct proportion to your self-respect. Use the asking process to practice self-honoring. Keep stretching in the direction of everything you want, and everything you want will stretch itself in your direction.

DOOR 4: YOU WILL MANIFEST AS MUCH AS YOU ARE WILLING TO INVEST IN.

The law of circulation is founded on the principle that prosperity must always keep moving. Prosperity can flow *to* you only to the extent that it flows *through* you. You cannot expect riches to simply fall in your lap by winning the lottery. People who strike it rich have invested of themselves. They have invested their time, thought, prayer, work, service, intention, vision, and money. Wealth is never an accident; it is always the result of energy moving toward a result.

If something is important for you to have, you must be willing to give of yourself to get it. Jesus told of two people—one who had much, but invested little, and another who had little, but invested all. The second person, Jesus explained, truly gave of himself and, therefore, merited a greater reward.

When your heart is strong about something, you are inspired to do whatever it takes to get it. Then your reward is double: your soul is fulfilled, and you enjoy material return as well.

DOOR 5: YOU WILL MANIFEST AS MUCH AS YOU ARE WILLING TO ACCEPT.

There are three components in the manifestation process: (1) you ask the Universe; (2) the Universe responds; and (3) you let it in. Many of us ask; the Universe always answers; but not so many of us are good at letting it in. Many people have a block to accepting their good when it shows up; therein lies the key to the final golden door.

My aunt often complained about her old couch. Several times I offered to buy her a new one, but she always refused. All she needed to do was say yes, and it was hers. Creating wealth is like driving with one foot on the gas pedal and one foot on the brake. You may be stepping on the gas by saying and doing things to attract what you want, but if your other foot is on the brake—resisting it when it comes—you will minimize or cancel the results of your efforts. The greatest secret of prosperity, the principle that would make the most difference if more people mastered it, is to *be a good receiver.*

Each of the five golden doors of prosperity has an affirmation which, if practiced, will unlock it.

1. *Everything I want is available now.*
2. *I deserve to have all that I want and need.*
3. *I ask for 100 percent of what I want 100 percent of the time.*

4. *To have all, I give all.*
5. *I am open and willing to receive everything my heart desires.*

For Reflection

1. What do you believe the Universe is capable of supplying for you? What do you believe it cannot supply? Would you be willing to regard the Universe as more abundant?

2. Are you asking for what you really want? Is there something you really want that you have not been asking for? Would you be willing to ask for it?

3. Is there something you want that you have been holding back on receiving? How could you be more open to receive it?

Are You Dreaming
Big Enough?

I saw a large billboard displaying photos of two bottles of liquor. One was a small bottle with the caption "Regular size." The other bottle was huge, many times larger than the tiny one—its caption said "Fantasize."

The only dreams worth entertaining are those greater than the life you are already living. When choosing a goal, make it outrageous. If it is something you have already done or think you may be able to do, you are thinking too small. Worthy dreams stretch us beyond our history and challenge our limits. They call us to live larger than we thought we were.

Here is a powerful exercise that will help you step into bigger shoes. On a piece of paper, write the heading "Know I Can." Under the heading, write the numbers 1 through 3 and record three goals you are confident you can accomplish, and probably will, within a matter of time. Below that section write "Maybe I Can." Then number 4 through 6, and list three projects you would like to do, but which would be a stretch to accomplish. Finally, write the heading "Outrageous," and for numbers 7 through 9, record the three most outlandish visions you can think of, the dreams that thrill you to consider, but at the moment you don't see how they could possibly happen.

Then read your list daily, spending about thirty seconds (a minute, if you are inspired) visualizing each goal. Hold each image clearly in mind, and get the feeling that you've already attained your objective.

Then, when each goal is accomplished, check it off your list—this is where the exercise really becomes fun! Your "imagineering" will attract support from the Universe, including outright miracles, through avenues you could never have predicted. As you complete checking off the first group, the second group will slide up to a level of possibility within your reach; the "Maybe I Can" section will become "Know I Can." Your excitement will further increase when the third group ascends to become the second; somehow the "Outrageous" becomes "Maybe I Can," and before too long, "Know I Can." Then you can add more to your "Maybe I Can" and "Outrageous" lists and watch them slide up like credits rolling at the end of a movie. Your role is to stay focused, keep visualizing, and remain open to receive more than you once thought you deserved.

I heard about a sales convention that centered on the theme "Think Big—Settle for More." Life gives us not what we struggle for, but what we allow. You can come to the ocean with a thimble, a bucket, or a tank truck, and you will take with you the volume of the container you bring.

One evening while I was leading a guided group meditation, I had a vision of a great light shining down on everyone in the room. The light represented the abundance of the universe, the vast love of God, replete with infinite good and blessings. In the vision, each person was sitting with a basket in his or her lap; some people held tiny baskets, and others huge ones. Those with small baskets were collecting a little light, and those with huge baskets were gathering a lot. Vast abundance was being offered to everyone, yet each person gathered according to the size of his or her basket.

William Blake boldly declared, "A man's reach should exceed his grasp, or else what's a heaven for?" Outrageous goals are valuable because they expand your belief system and carve wider neural pathways in your brain, by which your good may be delivered to you. Even if you do not achieve your highest goal immediately, you will attain far more than you would have if you had entertained a smaller dream. A friend told me, "I used to shoot for the moon, and I hit the mountains; now I shoot for the stars, and I'm hitting the moon."

Be humble enough to admit that you don't see your highest possibilities, yet confident enough to know that you can attain them. Even your most exalted insights glimpse but a tiny portion of the big picture. In 1949 an issue of *Popular Mechanics* magazine featured an article by an expert on the then-new field of computers. He predicted, "By the end of the century, computers may weigh as little as 1.5 tons." Little did he realize that by the turn of the millennium millions of people would manage their affairs from a tiny Palm Pilot, weighing just eight ounces—one five-thousandth the size of his prediction! The most respected visionary of his time erred by a factor of five thousand! Imagine that the good you can receive is five thousand times more wonderful than you can imagine, and you will take a significant step toward recognizing your potential as God already knows it.

For Reflection

1. On a scale of 1-10 (10 being the highest), how much does what you have represent what you want?

2. If your dream showed up tomorrow, would you be open and willing to accept it or would you still hold it at a distance?

3. Name several dreams you have had in the past that seemed outrageous when you first thought of them but eventually became a reality.

No Outside Factors

At a residential seminar I conducted, one participant found many things to complain about. She did not like her room, her roommate, or the retreat center, which she found to be too rustic and lacking in creature comforts. After the program, she went with another participant to stay at a luxury hotel and spa. There, her roommate reported, she also found many things not to her liking; everything was too expensive, the rooms were stuffy, and the people snobbish. In retrospect, it became clear that it was not the accommodations that brought this woman her experience, but the sense of discontent she brought to them.

We bring our own self with us wherever we go. We see the world not as it is, but as we are. We are subject not to what is "out there," but to the perceptual screens through which we filter what is out there. Everything you see has only the meaning you have given it. The world does not build your thoughts; your thoughts build the world.

I was visiting the home of a friend whose thirteen-year-old son announced he wanted to have a birthday party. "What kind of party would you like to have?" his mom asked him. "I want to have a casino party where we can all gamble!" the boy answered energetically.

I could see the energy in mom's face drop, for she believed that gambling is not a healthful pastime to teach children. Then, in the course of just a moment, I observed her energy shift; her eyes lit up as she responded, "That's a wonderful idea—all the kids can practice their math!"

This mother's rapid attitudinal pivoting demonstrates that the prime factor in success is *attitude.* We might say that there are two kinds of people in the world: *results* people and *excuses* people. *Results* people get the job done no matter what is going on around them, while *excuses* people have a million different reasons the job never gets done.

Several years ago I hired a fellow to do a project for me. When I called him to check on how it was going, he answered, "I've been really busy this week; next week I will handle it." When I phoned him the following week, he reported, "I haven't been feeling well, but things are looking up; next week I will have a good report for you." A week later he told me, "My girlfriend and I broke up, and I have been emotionally distraught but next week is the week." There was, however, no next week, for it became clear to me that this fellow gave his power away to everything outside himself and retained very little for himself. As Dr. Ken Blanchard, author of *One Minute Manager,* noted: "When you are interested in something, you do it only when it is convenient. When you are committed, you accept no excuses, only results."

Louis Pasteur revolutionized the medical world with his discovery of bacteria. On his deathbed, Pasteur confessed to a colleague: "I have made a big mistake. Now I realize that it is not bacteria that cause disease, but the medium with which the bacteria come into contact."

The implications of this insight are staggering! No germs can make you sick unless you are an available host. No virus, negative thought, or criminal can get to you unless your energy is aligned with them. When you are in a positive loving frame of mind, in harmony with your spiritual nature and the flow of life, you attract people and experiences that match this pure vibration. If, however, you get into a rut of negative thought and action incongruent with your joy, you become fair game for both physical and psychic germs.

Our primary responsibility is to stay connected to the stream of the love; then we have access to support, protection, and well-being we could never achieve through anxious struggle, manipulation, or fearful self-protection. When I was in Russia, I visited a church that housed an icon of Mother Mary that was venerated in the nineteenth century by the people in a small town. When a plague ravaged the surrounding region, it killed most of the people in all the other towns it touched. Yet no one in this town was taken by the disease. The environmental conditions were the same as those affecting the people who succumbed. Medical law and statistics would dictate that these devotees should have suffered the same fate—but they did not. I believe that the faith and devotion these people felt for Mother Mary kept them in a protective vibration, offering the bacteria no welcome host.

No outside factor can hurt you or save you. The next time you take all the factors into consideration, remember that no factor is more important than your awareness of your identity as a sovereign spiritual being.

For Reflection

1. To what external "authorities" have you given your power of happiness? (For example—money, men or women, landlord, parents, religion, doctors, news media)

2. How might your thoughts and beliefs be attracting events that seem to be issuing from outside factors?

3. How might you shift your attitude or actions so you take your power back and live from your own choices rather than the choices others would make for you?

Pray Outside the Box

*I*n my seminars, I lead an exercise called "My Ideal Day." If you were participating, I would ask you to take a piece of paper and write down in detail the most wonderful day you can imagine. The only requirement for each activity you list is that you would choose it from a sense of joy and delight rather than routine or obligation. When seminar participants do this process, they become very animated and usually come up with inspiring ideas about how they could actually create such a day—and life.

In one seminar, a woman read aloud her essay describing her ideal day. After relating many delicious experiences, she read: "And then in the evening, my husband and I go into Toronto to see our favorite opera performed by world-renowned singers. We ride in a big limousine, which allows my husband to stretch out his arthritic legs."

When I heard her words, something struck me as out of tune. "Why," I asked her, "would you include arthritis in your ideal day?"

"Well," she answered, "I guess my husband has had arthritis for so long that I can't imagine him without it."

"Perhaps," I suggested, "that is one of the reasons the condition has persisted."

We must be careful to build our experiences around

our visions, rather than building our visions around our experiences. *Your history is not your destiny.* Imagine a prisoner doing the "Ideal Day" exercise. "I get up in the morning, go out into the prison yard, and shoot some hoops with the other inmates," he might envision. "Then I come into the prison cafeteria and find they are serving meat loaf for lunch . . ."

But why include prison in the vision at all? If you have been in prison for a long time (metaphorically speaking), you may have a hard time envisioning yourself out of it. But if you can, you are well on your way to freedom. Any vision that includes the prison is not doing you justice.

While I was a guest on a radio talk show interview featuring my book *Handle With Prayer,* a caller shared an inspiring story. "When my daughter was scheduled to go for surgery, I asked my prayer group to pray for a positive outcome to the surgery," he recounted. "At the prayer group, someone asked: 'Why accept the surgery as a done deal? Let's pray that your daughter be healed without the surgery.' So we prayed for a natural healing. When I took my daughter for her next exam, the doctor informed me that her condition had cleared up and she no longer needed the surgery."

I cite this story not to influence you against surgery, but to invite you to pray outside the box. Sometimes we do not ask for what we want, but for what we expect we can get, or what others tell us we should have. But if what we expect is less than what we want, we have sold ourselves, our prayers, and our God short. Abraham has said, "Never accept any reality unless it includes all of what you want."

To avoid booby-trapping your visions or affirmations, weed out elements contrary to your goal. Always think and speak about where you want to end up rather than where you are coming from. For example, never try to lose weight; seek to gain fitness. Do not seek to avoid aging; instead, tap into your sense of youthful vitality. And don't try to get out of a bad relationship; get a clear picture of the kind of relationship you would like, and ask the current relationship to transform or a better one to show up. Never say anything about yourself that you would not like to come true; state the best about yourself rather than what you fear or resist. Your powerful subconscious mind tends to manifest any picture you hold, so make it a good one.

Your words are the least part of your prayers and affirmations. The purpose of words in prayer and affirmation is to focalize your energy. God, which is Spirit, reads and responds to your energy flow. So if you are saying "I want" with your words, but "I can't" with your energy, "can't" wins. You can't be immersed in complaint about what is not working and get things to work. You simply can't get there from here. The Universe is not fooled by words, and don't you be, either. Another name for God is "Yes." Whatever you focus on is "yes." If you are pushing against something, you are energetically saying yes to it. So be sure to focus on what you want, not what you don't want. Attention is investment.

I often see people defeat their own goals by defending their problems. In some counseling sessions I make suggestions to clients, and then they tell me all the reasons the suggestions will not work. When this happens repeatedly, I realize the clients have more of an investment in being right about their limits than in having what they want. They are not ready to receive their requests. When they have more to say about where they want to be than where they are, they will have their dreams.

You, too, shall have your dream, but you must be in harmony with it before it can show up. You must become an advocate for your possibilities rather than your shortcomings. Get on your own team. If you were a sports team coach who discovered some players did not know which way to run with the ball, you would not let them on the field. In life, your best players are all the thoughts, words, feelings, and actions that match your ideal. Send only them onto the field, and watch them score big time.

For Reflection

1. Do the "My Ideal Day" exercise listed above. Write down the best possible day you can imagine—in glorious detail, in the present tense—including the joyful feelings you experience. Include only the elements you would have in your ideal day by your choice.

2. Is there any problematic situation that keeps persisting in your experience? Are you spending more energy, thoughts, and words on what is wrong than on how you would like it to turn out? What should you do to reverse your energy in favor of your goal?

3. For a day, week, or month, watch what comes out of your mouth after you say, "I am . . ." Try to voice only the attributes you would like to have more of.

Toxic Thoughts

One morning soon after I moved my office to a country setting, I stepped outside for a breath of fresh air. There I noticed a large, gray pig poking its nose through the hedges between my office and the house next door. It was not our first surprise since moving out of town.

"Hey, Samantha, there's a pig out here!" I called to my office manager.

"Oh, yes, watch for its mother, the dog," she called back.

"What?"

"Our neighbors found the pig in a field just after it was born. The only animal role model it had was the dog. The pig thinks the dog is its mother; he follows her around everywhere."

Just then a big, black dog emerged from the yard. The pig nuzzled up to her and followed her home.

As I stepped back into the office, I began to consider that perhaps our predicament is not so different from the pig's. We have accepted an identity unlike who we are. We are spiritual beings, and we think our bodies limit us. We are whole, and we think we are broken. We came to live a magnificent destiny, and we accept the insecurities modeled by those who came before us.

Pop psychology has coined the term *toxic relation-*

ships and made us very aware of them. Books, talk shows, and therapy sessions are buzzing with references to toxic parents, toxic children, and toxic partners. The notion is that some people are just not healthful for us to be around, and we should avoid them.

Okay, that may be true—but we're not done yet. Yes, other people may be involved in our discomfort, but they are not the cause of it. To truly be free, we must go deeper. We must discover and heal the thought patterns we hold that draw such people to us and color our view of self as victim. Ultimately, our goal is not to get rid of the people who bother us, but to grow beyond the thoughts that drag us down. Ultimately, we must upgrade our consciousness until we behold perfection where we thought it was absent.

We are responsible for what we see; what we see is a result of the vision we use to see it. Happiness and sadness proceed not from external sources, but from the judgments we hold about people and events. From the highest perspective, the notion of toxic *anything* out there is a trick of the mind; it is the ego, or separated self, trying to convince us that we are victims of the world we see rather than the chooser of the thoughts which create that world.

Claiming ownership of toxic thoughts does not mean we must force ourselves to stay in abusive or painful situations. It means that we can't afford to identify other people as the source of our problems. We have every right to remove ourselves from self-defeating situations and put ourselves in a more healthful environment; but for God's sake don't turn anyone into a devil—that's how inquisitions and holocausts get started.

Looking In for Number One

Each day brings us a thousand opportunities to behold the world God made rather than the one we superimposed over it with toxic thoughts. When I drive to my office now, I go around a curve in the road next to a house where a family of peacocks lives. One morning as I came around the curve, a peahen was leading a queue of babies across the road. I stopped to enjoy the striking azure color of the little birds, reflected brilliantly in the morning sunlight. I marveled at the splendor before me and thanked God for the opportunity to start my day with this magnificent display.

On the other side of the peacocks, another car was stopped. The driver of that car was not so pleased with the parade. She was in a hurry, and the peacock march was simply a source of frustration. The woman sat there, fuming, making scowling expressions as she waited for the peacocks to cross. As soon as the birds reached the other side of the road, she floored the gas pedal and screeched off.

How interesting, I thought, that the two of us came upon the same scene and interpreted it in entirely opposite ways. I viewed it as a gift from God, and she saw it as a nuisance. "Toxic animals," she might have mumbled.

Everything is what we make it or, more accurately, what we let it be. If we allow everything to be what it is, we will ultimately find the divine in everything. That is why we must let ourselves be what we are. We cannot afford to judge against anyone, including ourselves, for in doing so we miss the blessing at hand. The only real toxicity we need to be concerned about is the poisonous line of thought that defines life through the filter of fear rather than love. If we can learn to love enough, the thought of blaming anyone else for our pain will be as foreign to us as a pig thinking it is a dog.

For Reflection

1. What beliefs, attitudes, or programs did you pick up from your parents or early teachers that your own experience has shown you to be erroneous?

2. Are there any people whom you regard as "toxic"? Is there a way you can reframe them in your thinking so you can accept them as they are? What gifts or lessons do they offer you?

3. How do you think God regards people you see as toxic?

Don't Follow Me

I saw a bumper sticker warning, "Don't follow me— I'm following my bliss." What good advice! How much more creative and successful would your life be if you remained true to yourself rather than imitating the paths chosen by others?

In Monty Python's hilarious film *Life of Brian,* a scofflaw during the time of Jesus eludes Roman soldiers by disguising himself as a pundit. Brian steps onto a soapbox in the town square and spouts mock words of wisdom. As soon as the soldiers depart, Brian makes a beeline for the city limits, only to discover a crowd of students following him. Soon the throng grows from hundreds to thousands, begging their master to teach them. Finally, Brian turns and chides them, "I'm not your master—just go away!"

"But, master!" a voice cries out from the crowd, "tell us *how* we should go away."

Many of us have given our power, minds, and money to people who we believe can tell us how to live. And many teachers have given us good advice. But advice is useful only if it resonates deep within us in a place that feels like home. So the teacher did not give us anything we did not already have; he or she just pointed us to what we already knew.

A false guru is someone who sits by the bank of a river selling bottles of river water. Anyone could just go directly to the river and draw water without going through a middle party. There are two kinds of gurus: those who get their students hooked on bottled water and keep upping the price, and those who show their students how to get their own water. The best teachers are those who work themselves out of a job.

Years ago I got involved with a cult led by a teacher who claimed to be enlightened. The students in this organization worshipped the teacher more than the teachings, and I went right along with the hype. I gave my power away to this man, and I did lots of things to fit in with the crowd. But every time I fit in, I sold out. Eventually a scandal revealed that the teacher had been lying to the students and engaging in covert activities contrary to his teachings.

When the debacle became public, I felt shocked, ripped off, and angry. I blamed the teacher for fooling me. After some introspection, however, I realized that I had fooled myself. If I had been true to myself, I never would have become one of the sheep. Then I began to appreciate the experience. I realized that the purpose of my involvement with the teacher was not the lessons he gave, but for me to learn to follow my own spirit rather than the herd. Suddenly the whole process became immensely valuable to me, and I laughed about it. It was worth the experience to learn how to respect my sacred Self more than external authority.

Occasionally I receive a request from someone who wants to represent my work. One woman wanted me to

certify her to teach a course based on one of my books. I
asked her which book she wanted to teach. She told me,
"Dare to Be Yourself." The whole idea seemed ironically
humorous to me. She wanted me to authorize her to teach
people how to be themselves. I told her that the only way
she could teach such a course successfully was to be herself, and she certainly didn't need my permission to do
that. No one will ever represent me like I do, and I would
never attempt to replicate you. We both have too much
individual worth and beauty to rubber stamp what God
created in immaculate brilliance.

Yet most people spend much of their lives trying to
follow in the footsteps of others. Eventually they become
frustrated and disheartened, for they have missed out on
the only thing that brings true reward—living authentically. Emerson declared, "Imitation is suicide." More
recently, the pop group Sister Hazel sang, "If you want to
be somebody else, change your mind." Roger Ebert, in
reviewing a particularly unconvincing movie, noted, "It is
painful to watch actors speaking dialogue that is clearly
inferior to the thoughts that must be running through
their minds at the very same time." We have all been those
actors, speaking lines designated for other people. The
bad movie goes on until you say: "Wait a minute! I've gotten into someone else's movie! I want my own back!"

Then you recognize that your guide is never another
person. Your only trustworthy guide is your own bliss.
The God within you will never lead you astray. The same
God that guided Jesus, Moses, Buddha, Mohammed, and
every other great teacher will guide you. You can't afford
to follow a photocopied God. Do not settle for another

person's truth. That person can inspire you, but you must claim your own direct connection with divinity.

If you are tempted to deliver God or Truth to others, tread with caution, friend. The greatest gift you can give others is the inspiration to find wholeness within themselves. Heaven has no seats for groupies. Don't be one and don't seek one. Seek the light, and that is all you will find. Is there anything else you would really want?

We walk side by side, but each of us must follow our own truth. There are many roads to the mountaintop; the only one that will take you all the way is the one with your name on it.

For Reflection

1. Do you tend to put people on a pedestal? What happens when you do?

2. Have you ever put your intuition aside to follow someone who turned out to be an impostor? What did you learn? Would you be as likely to repeat the experience?

3. Consider the teachers you most respect. What do they have in common?

Rude Awakening

"My whole life changed when I injured my hand," Judy told me. "I lost my career as a hospital technician, and then my house, and I found myself alone for many hours a day. It was really a rude awakening!"

Judy's choice of words struck me. "You've told me about the rude part," I responded. "What about the awakening?"

"Well, there were some major blessings," she admitted. "I quit running around like a crazy person. When I was in my job, I was on call 24/7. I would be driving home after my shift at the hospital, my beeper would go off, and I would turn right around. Then, after I couldn't work, I began to think about what I really wanted to do with my life. I decided to go back to college. Now I'm studying psychology, something I have always wanted to do. And I have more quality time with my kids. In the long run, I think I'm better off."

The Chinese written character for the word *crisis* is a combination of two other characters: *danger* plus *opportunity.* Every crisis could lead to a result that might hurt you, but it could also empower you. The outcome depends not on the events that have occurred, but on what you make of them. If you can find the blessing, you are on your way to being better off than when you started.

In his book *Positive Disintegration,* a psychologist named Dombrowski explained how a nervous breakdown is a very healthful experience. It serves as a safety valve for a life on the verge of blowing up. When Dr. Dombrowski's patients' lives fell apart, they had to step back from self-defeating patterns and reach inward for the selves they had lost sight of. They had to admit that the way they were living was not working and then choose a more meaningful path. So, their breakdown became a breakthrough.

All change is good, and everything serves. If life seems to be against us, it is only because we are looking through a distorted perceptual screen. One very worthwhile question to ask of a challenge is, "How might this experience strengthen me?" Regard the difficulty as your friend, and you will discover it is not a curse from the devil, but a gift from God.

As Judy described the changes resulting from her hand injury, she added, "The thing that drove me craziest was when my 'spiritual' friends asked, 'How did you create this?' If my hand had been healthy, I would have punched them! While I was hurting physically and emotionally, the last thing I wanted was to feel guilty about doing something stupid."

Hmmm. "I would like to ask you the same question with a different twist," I told Judy. "How *in wisdom* did you create the event? How, *through loving yourself,* did you draw such an experience into your life?"

Looking In for Number One

"The truth be told," Judy answered, "I was quite unhappy with my life the way it was, but I didn't want to confront my fears about making a change. I needed a dramatic event to get my attention. If I had been challenged in a more gentle way, I probably would have just gone on clinging to my old security blankets, meanwhile dying inside a little bit more every day."

Dramatic events are orchestrated by an organization called In-Your-Face-Productions. This company writes scripts and hires actors that are so loud and obvious that you can't possibly miss the message. They specialize in wake-up calls. I had a little alarm clock that would beep very softly at first and then beep progressively louder until I had no choice but to awaken. Such is life: if you don't respond to the whisper, you get the slap.

The important thing to remember when confronted with In-Your-Face-Productions is that *it is not a punishment*. It is a *gift*. The only thing more cruel than turning your old life upside down would be to let it go on the way it was not working. Such is grace.

A Course in Miracles explains that the word *challenge* is a misnomer, for it implies there is a chance we may fail—and that is impossible. We may make mistakes or experience setbacks along the way, but a setback is really a *setup*. Often a setback motivates us to rethink how we have been approaching our situation and, ultimately, makes us more determined to succeed. So, a temporary failure can become a stepping-stone to ultimate achievement.

For every rude, there is an awakening. For every upset, there is a setup. For every danger, there is an opportunity. When you are fully committed to finding the good, the love, and the presence of Spirit in every situation, you will see your life as God sees it. Then you can forget about the rude and keep the awakening.

For Reflection

1. Have you had a rude awakening? What was rude? What was the awakening?

2. Think of an error you have made. How, *in wisdom*, did you create it?

3. Consider a setback you have experienced. How might it be a setup to ultimately succeed?

Fair or Powerful?

I visited a church where a husband and wife team of ministers conducted the services each Sunday morning. At the outset of their ministry, the couple took turns delivering the weekly sermon. Then a pattern became obvious: On the Sundays when the wife, who is a very eloquent speaker, addressed the congregation, large numbers of people showed up. On the alternate Sundays, when the husband spoke, about half the number of congregants attended.

When the couple became aware of the disparity in attendance, they decided that no matter how many people showed up, the fair thing to do was to continue to give each minister an equal opportunity to speak. But as time went on, the disparity deepened—the number of listeners to the wife increased, and the number of listeners to the husband decreased. Moreover, the church was facing financial challenges.

The ministers revisited their agreement and conceded that the Universe was giving them a clear message. It was obvious that the wife was to be the Sunday speaker. Although the husband's ego was bruised, he admitted that he did not really enjoy speaking, and there were other aspects of the ministry he enjoyed more, such as working with the youth group. So the couple divided their re-

174

sponsibilities according to their personal strengths and the maximal results they could each manifest. Soon the Sunday attendance shot up every week, the youth group attendance swelled, and the church stepped into unprecedented prosperity.

Success does not issue from what looks fair on paper; it proceeds from where the most truth lives. (Native Americans ask of any plan, "Will it grow corn?") If it works, it is fair; if it is not working, it is not fair. Each of us prospers individually when we are true to our own talents and heart's desires, and the same principle applies to relationships and organizations. What you manifest depends not on a set of stock external rules, but the consciousness you are holding. You are always getting what you deserve by virtue of how much you love what you are doing and how much your outer actions match your inner intentions.

When a friend of mine set out to work in a program to help inner-city residents, she began with lofty idealism and a sense of injustice that these poor people were downtrodden by society. "If only underprivileged people had money like the rich," she muttered, "they would have an equal chance to succeed." After a few years in the program, however, she changed her tune. "I don't think it is money they need," she admitted. "What they really need is the knowledge of what to do with the money." Regularly, she saw people spend their paychecks and government subsidies on liquor and drugs. Very few people used money to uplift themselves. She discovered that the best way to help people who live in poverty is to reveal to them their inner riches and help them discover their self-

worth. Then they are in a strong position to use their resources for self-improvement that proceeds from the inside out.

A minister recounted that before a Sunday service a woman came into his church and told him she was going to commit suicide because she didn't have any money for breakfast for herself and her child. The minister gave her $25 to buy some groceries. The woman came back after the service and complained that she was still hungry. "What did you do with the $25 I gave you?" he asked. "I bought lottery tickets," she answered.

There is a theory that if all the money in the world were redistributed equally among all the people of the world, within a short time the money would be back in its original hands in the original proportions. This is not because life is unjust, but because it is totally just—each of us manifests according to our own consciousness. Usually when we think it is more money we need, what we really need is more consciousness. We do not need to ante up; we need to wake up.

Life is always fair, but it is fair according to principles that run far deeper than the societal rules by which we have been taught to evaluate fairness. The law of consciousness supercedes all human-created laws. As you think, so shall it be. Life is fair in that the situations around us provide a perfect reflection of the thoughts, beliefs, attitudes, and expectations we hold. The moment we recognize the utter justice of our manifestations, we become extremely powerful, for we realize that we are imbued with the power to cocreate with God. "Here is a blank canvas and a palette of vibrant paints," the Universe says to us. "You are free to paint any picture you wish. And if you don't like what you have painted, you are free to paint a new and more rewarding one."

When you are true to yourself and your gifts, everything falls into place. Actions aligned with inner vision create manifestations that are both powerful and fair to everyone.

For Reflection

1. Are you currently in or observing any situation that you believe is unfair? Can you see how the situation is a manifestation of the inner attitudes or beliefs that you or others are holding?

2. Consider a situation in which you believe that your life, or other people's, would be better if you or they had a certain thing (e.g., money, car, home). What kind of consciousness would you or they have to step into in order to get, keep, and make productive use of this thing?

3. What does it mean to be a cocreator with God?

Who Knows?

s a young girl, Toni wanted more than anything to become an artist. She enjoyed working with many media and fantasized about the day when she would make an exciting career expressing her talents. At the age of twelve, Toni took an art class with her sister Jackie. At the end of the course, the teacher, Mr. Jamison, took Toni's mother aside and told her, "Jackie is very talented, but I don't have much hope for Toni—she erases too much."

At first Toni felt crushed, but soon her disappointment shifted into determination; her teacher's criticism only made her more intent on succeeding. So she took up pen and ink drawings—a medium in which erasing is impossible. Years later Toni exhibited her work at a street fair.

At the exhibit, many people complimented Toni on her renderings, but one man's comments really got her attention. He shook her hand enthusiastically and told her, "These are the most fantastic pen and ink drawings I have ever seen!" Toni chuckled inwardly to receive this compliment from Mr. Jamison.

For whom do you live and work? Whom do you strive to impress? Do you express yourself to please others or yourself? Do you evaluate your creations by external opinions or your inner knowingness? Do you allow the words or reactions of others to make and break you, or do you find nourishment through your inner spirit?

Often professional critics are poor judges of quality or talent. After the film *Patch Adams* came to theaters, I read the movie review section in a popular entertainment magazine, where a half-dozen prestigious movie critics rated current releases. The grades that *Patch Adams* received were the worst of the lot, ranging from "C" to a dismal "F." Then I noticed another column that did not reflect the grades of professional reviewers, but those of many moviegoers who saw the film. In this column, *Patch Adams* received an "A"—the highest grade of all the movies.

This disparity speaks a very important lesson: the only people critics speak for are themselves. Their opinions often bear little reflection of the value that viewers ascribe to a movie. (The great composer Jean Sibelius noted, "No statue has ever been erected to a critic.") If you want to know the worth of a film or a book, ask someone with a value system similar to your own. Better yet, see or read it yourself. If you were the only person in the world who thought this movie or book was great, would you have the courage and integrity to hold firm to your appreciation?

The outer world is not the place to look for your values and answers; they must ultimately issue from within. Most people do not think for themselves; they simply go along with mass beliefs. Popular opinion changes with the wind and often is not guided by wisdom. One day as I entered a cafeteria line at an airport, I saw a large sign declaring, "It is impolite to pass others in the cafeteria line." Okay, I thought, I can live with that rule. The next time I visited that cafeteria, the sign had been changed. This time it said, "It is acceptable to pass others in the cafeteria line." Somehow, in just a short time, the rules of politeness and acceptability had changed.

A Course in Miracles asks us to remember, "I am under no laws but God's." Within you is an infallible guide to right action, relationship, creativity, and self-expression. When your creations are aligned with your inner being, you have limitless power to manifest them, and the Universe will support you in miraculous ways.

When I finished writing my first book, *The Dragon Doesn't Live Here Anymore*, I mailed the manuscript to several publishers, all of whom rejected it. Then I made phone contact with one successful publisher of self-help books. He asked me, "What's this book about?" I told him, "The healing power of love and forgiveness." The man scowled and suggested, "Write something more dynamic." Quickly I realized that if anyone was going to stand behind my book, it would have to be me.

I borrowed some money and set out to publish the book myself. I found a printer, made a deal, and wrote the largest check I had ever written in my life. As I was walking out of the printer's office, he told me, "You know they say you don't make any money until your third book." I couldn't believe what I was hearing! Here I was, a hopeful young man who had just invested a great deal of someone else's money, and this guy was throwing water on my dream! There was no way I was going to accept his "law." Spontaneously I answered, "Perhaps that is what they say, but what they don't know is that my agent is God."

The book went on to sell out its first printing in a short time and quickly became a best-seller in the inspirational market. It has sold over 200,000 copies to date and is still going strong. "They" did not know Whom "they" were dealing with.

After Dr. Wayne Dyer's book *Your Erroneous Zones* became an international blockbuster, an excerpt was incorporated in a college entrance reading comprehension test. For fun, Dr. Dyer took the test himself. You can imagine his consternation when he received a grade of "B." When Dr. Dyer asked the graders how they explained the fact that the author of the excerpt achieved only a "B," they answered, "Sometimes even the author does not fully understand what he wrote."

I suggest that the author does understand his own writing, and you understand your own destiny. There is a wisdom within you that is fully aware of who you are, where you are to go, and what you are to do. No one knows your purpose better than you, and you are the only one who can live it.

For Reflection

1. Have you ever turned away from something you wanted to do because someone thought you should not do it? How do you feel about that now? What did you learn?

2. Have you ever gone on to do something you believed in, even if no one else agreed with you? What did you learn?

3. Name a movie or piece of music or art that was panned by the critics, but which you thought was magnificent. Do you need agreement to feel validated, or is your own inner knowing enough?

Numb and Number

I have a confession to make. I watched the movie *Dumb and Dumber.* What's even more embarrassing: I liked it. Even beyond belief: I found at least two metaphysical lessons in the film which prove that God *must* be everywhere.

The movie includes a scene in which Lloyd (played by Jim Carrey) declares his love to Mary, the woman of his dreams. After he lays it on the line, Lloyd asks Mary, "What would you say are my chances with you—one in ten?" Mary thinks for a moment and answers bluntly, "More like one in a million."

Lloyd becomes very serious and begins to breathe deeply. Mary steps back in fear that he may lash out at her. Instead, a huge grin spreads over Lloyd's face and he gleefully shouts: "Wow! I have a chance!"

Sometimes dumb is smarter. Sometimes what appears to be naiveté is really openness to all possibilities in a limitless universe. Sometimes people who know all the facts and statistics and probabilities are not as smart as someone who doesn't know what he or she can't do. Sometimes savvy backfires and innocence triumphs.

And sometimes dumb is simply missing out on a possibility right in front of you. In a later scene in the movie, Lloyd and his sidekick Harry (it's hard to tell who is

183

dumber) have exhausted their search for true love and find themselves dejected and stranded along the side of a desert road. Suddenly a busload of bikini-clad babes pulls over and three awesome beauties descend. "Say," one cutie asks them coyly, "do you guys know where we can find two men who would like to travel with us for a few months and spread oil all over us before our suntan lotion demonstrations?"

Quickly Dumb (or was it Dumber?) answers: "Sure! There's a town three miles down the road that way." The babes, disappointed the duo didn't take the hint, chug off, leaving our antiheroes in a cloud of dust. Then Lloyd turns to his buddy and remarks: "You know, Harry, some guys have all the luck. I hope and pray that one day the same good fortune might come to us."

Sometimes the opportunity you have been waiting for is tapping you on the shoulder. It may even be *shaking* you by the shoulders, yelling *"Helloooo?"* But if you have a preconceived notion about how it should arrive or if you are stuck in complaining that it has not arrived, you may not recognize it. The answer to your prayer may be rushing to you from all angles—but if your attention is elsewhere, you might miss it.

When I visited Egypt, our tour group arrived at the Great Pyramid of Giza early one morning while a thick fog still clung to the desert. When our tour bus pulled to a stop, someone in our group asked, "Where is the Great Pyramid?" The tour guide laughed and answered, "A few feet in front of you." If we were any closer, we would have driven into it! Yet the fog was so thick that we had no idea it was right there. The Great Pyramid!

We tend to be fooled by appearances, even while divine order is right beside us. If your thoughts are fogbound, you may not recognize the treasure that awaits you but inches away. Problems are what you see when you take your eye off your goal. You may pray or work toward a dream without apparent results. The key word here is *apparent*. Sometimes it takes a while for our dreams to be delivered, often with good reason. We must trust that Spirit's invisible methodology supersedes our own ideas of how and when things should happen.

When I was writing my book *Lifestyles of the Rich in Spirit,* I set a self-imposed deadline by which I would finish the book. (The word *deadline* is apt here; often it is the noose that strangles our spirits.) As the time approached, I worked more and more feverishly, with diminishing returns. The quality of the material was weakened and I became ill. On the day I had chosen for the book's completion, I found myself in bed with the flu; I had run down my batteries, and the Universe forced me to stop trying to buck the tide of life.

Fortunately, I got the message and surrendered. I gave up my idea of how and when the book should be finished, and I consciously turned the process over to God. I continued to work on the book at a more relaxed pace, and within a short time the quality of the material returned to a high standard. Eventually the book was published, and then I understood why it had to wait: during the time I continued to write it, I experienced a great deal of spiritual growth. Ultimately, my new level of consciousness was imbued in the pages. If I had forced the book to come out according to my time schedule, the book would

not have been any improvement over my earlier writing; it would have just been similar material in a different form. But what is the use of doing the same thing again? Now that I see the process retrospectively, I am glad that I waited and produced a superior offering.

Because we are created in the image and likeness of God, we cannot be dumb; but because we have free will, we can be numb. Kabir quipped, "I laugh when I hear that the fish in the water is thirsty." At this moment we are literally swimming in a sea of blessings; let us say yes to love.

For Reflection

1. Can you think of a time when the Universe was offering you a gift but you did not notice it? How would you handle that situation, knowing what you now know?

2. Is there a situation in your life now that you feel impatient to have manifested? Is it possible that divine timing is in progress even though you don't realize it? How might you help yourself by relaxing and trusting?

3. What is the meaning of Jesus' teaching: "Judge not by appearances, but judge by right judgment"?

Tolerate or Embrace?

*A*t a holistic health center, I met a psychotherapist who focuses on his patients' emotions. "I try to get my patients to accept and appreciate all their feelings," Leonard told me. "I teach them that there is no such thing as a bad feeling; anger, fear, and sadness all bring us valuable opportunities to awaken and grow. We must embrace all that we are and experience."

Later I overheard another man telling someone about Leonard's work. "I met a therapist this morning who does 'feelings' therapy. He says we should tolerate ourselves."

Tolerate? I hadn't heard Leonard say anything about *tolerating* ourselves. When I think of toleration, I picture forcing myself to put up with something that is obnoxious and abhorrent; just tolerate it for a while and hope it goes away soon. If you tolerate yourself, you must think you are really repulsive. If you're just tolerating yourself, you don't know who you are. And if you're just tolerating someone else, you've missed who he or she is.

Our deepest need is to embrace ourselves, to rejoice in what we are and magnify it to the highest degree. Let us not define any part of ourselves as dark or evil. Walt Whitman boldly declared, "Welcome is every organ and attribute of me . . . not an inch or a particle of an inch is vile, and one shall not be less familiar than the rest."

In the Arthur Miller play *After the Fall,* a character offers a poetic soliloquy: "I dreamed I had a child, and even in the dream I saw that it was my life, and it was an idiot, and I ran away. But it always crept into my lap again, clutched at my clothes. Until I thought, if I could kiss it, whatever in it was my own, perhaps I could sleep. And I bent over the broken face, and it was horrible . . . but I kissed it. I think that one must finally take one's life into one's arms."

There comes a point at which we must finally take our lives in our arms. We do not need more force, pressure, threats, or intimidation. Children do not respond well to military tactics, and your spirit does not thrive in the presence of attack—especially when you are attacking yourself. But we *do* flourish in the midst of kindness, tenderness, and caring. Do not say anything to yourself or about yourself that you would not say about a precious child with whose life you are entrusted.

I remember dropping a juice bottle in my kitchen and hearing myself say aloud, "You clumsy jerk," as it broke. I was stunned. I would never say that to a child, so why would I say it to myself? That experience reminded me how important it is to respect myself even when I do not look or feel my best.

If everything else you have tried is not working, try love. Before taking any further action, sit down and enfold yourself in a mantle of tender caring and then radiate the same to everyone concerned. Armed with love, you will work miracles. Because love is our true nature, everything in the universe must respond to it.

Anatole France advised: "Make love now, by night and by day, in winter and in summer . . . You are in the world for that and the rest of life is nothing but vanity, illusion, waste. There is only one science, love, one riches, love, only one policy, love. To make love is all the law and the prophets."

We have studied and experimented with many "laws," but they are not truly laws unless they work consistently, in all situations. Love is the law behind all others. It has predictable effects and everlasting benefits. It is the law that outlives all others, for it is the purpose of our existence.

For Reflection

1. Who is the most loving person you have ever known? What attracted you to this person, and what kind of effect does he or she have on you and others?

2. Think of a situation that may be challenging or troubling you. How would your favorite loving person approach it?

3. What kinds of unkind things do you say about yourself— and *to* yourself—mentally or verbally? How could you reframe the situations you judge, so that you take a loving and accepting attitude toward yourself? What kind words could you use to replace the harsh and judgmental statements?

Lightheart

While perusing the hieroglyphics in an ancient Egyptian tomb, I discovered a painting showing a set of scales, like the scales of justice. On one side of the scales rested a feather, and on the other, a human heart. Near the scales, a godly entity looked on, along with an ugly monsterlike animal.

Our Egyptologist explained that this image depicted the Egyptian concept of the Day of Judgment. When someone died, according to the ancient legend, forty-two gods would accuse the person of various sins. If the person could deny these sins—while keeping his heart as light as a feather—he would be admitted to heaven and enjoy eternal life. If he could not deny these sins with a light heart, the nasty-looking jackal entity would devour him and send him to . . . well, you know.

If I were a fire-and-brimstone minister, I could have a field day with this scenario. But I am a teacher of forgiveness, and I will have my own field day with it.

Can you recognize your innocence when others are trying to convince you that you are guilty? In *The Four Agreements*, Don Miguel Ruiz advises, "Don't take anything personally." At the deepest level, we are all innocent. None of us has done anything that would cause us for even a moment to lose the love of God or deserve damnation. To the contrary, we are born of light and unto light we return. And even while we walk through a world that constantly denies and distracts us from our wholeness, we remain the light. If we practice forgiveness and self-honoring, we can remember our divine nature and extend this gift to others.

When faced with a demanding situation, can you keep your heart as light as a feather? Can you laugh your way through challenges and maintain an attitude freer than fear? When confronted with the judgments and poisonous projections of others, can you remember that all is well?

One of my favorite movie characters is played by Gene Wilder in *Stir Crazy*. Harry is a perpetually happy-go-lucky fellow with a knack for turning every experience into a gift. When Harry is thrown into prison for a crime he did not commit, the prison officials try to break his positive attitude. But they can't. The guards hang Harry by his wrists for several days and return to find him with a huge smile across his face. "Thank you, oh, thank you!" he exclaims exuberantly as they untie him. "You've finally solved my back problem!" Next, the officials lock Harry in a little hot box under the sweltering sun. When they extract him days later, he begs, "Oh, please, give me just one more day—I was just starting to get into myself." Finally, they throw Harry into a cell with Grossberger, a 350-pound, crazed murderer whom the toughest criminals avoid like the plague. When the guards return, they find Harry and Grossberger on the floor laughing over a game of cards. Harry keeps choosing joy, and his world lines up with his best interests.

We can apply the lightheart principle to our relationships as well. Many of us have gotten bogged down analyzing our love affairs to death. But we cannot experience love by dissecting it; the nature of love is openness, play, delight, and celebration. It is about supporting one another to be ever more passionately creative. Yes, you may have challenging moments, but relationship is not supposed to consume your soul; it is intended to enrich it. My friend Dr. Chuck Spezzano wrote a book titled *If It Hurts, It Isn't Love*. If you are in pain more than joy, analyzing more than celebrating, or finding more fault than beauty in yourself and your partner, you have drifted into dangerous waters and you must set sail for port as quickly as you can. Relationship was not created as an arena to project need and blame and judgment, but as a safe and sacred space to grow beyond guilt and fear. Yes, upsets may happen, but there is life beyond processing. How many times can you have the same argument? Redefine your relationship as a venue to gladden your heart, and you will find healing where you once wandered lonely in a hellish battlefield. Practice rising in love rather than falling, and you are on your way home.

Throughout your day, as often as possible, take a heart reading. Ask yourself: "In this moment, is my heart light or heavy? Am I pandering to fear or proceeding from my inner strength? Have I given my power to appearances, or do I remember the Truth?"

The lesson is the same for the lighthearted Egyptian, Harry the prisoner, and you and me: Enjoy your life. Everything else is detail. Forget about the ugly monster waiting to devour you; he is a figment of somebody else's imagination. Your own imagination can take you to far brighter places.

We have been taught that Spirit and matter are disconnected, but they are not. Matter is an expression of Spirit, and in the end, the only thing that matters is Spirit.

For Reflection

1. At this moment, is your heart light as a feather? If not, what is making it heavy? Can you find a way to lighten up?

2. Consider several people who love you and anyone who does not. Can you see how each of these people has generated his or her own experience of you?

3. Consider the people you love and those you do not like. Can you see how you have generated your experience of them?

Relationship 101

*J*ust down the road from my house lives a saint. He does not wear a turban or issue cosmic prophecies. Neither does he deliver discourses, heal lepers, or cast out demons. He is not attired in a white robe, but a green hooded sweatshirt. This saint gives blessings not from a pulpit, but from a wheelchair.

Raymond sits in his wheelchair at the end of his driveway, grinning and waving to every car that passes his house. I do not know Raymond's age, astrological sign, or how he got to be in a wheelchair, and he knows nothing about me. Yet our relationship is deeply intimate and extraordinarily rewarding.

When I pass Raymond, I am often on the way to an appointment. Sometimes I am running a bit late. My mind is immersed in the hubbub of life. When I see Raymond, however, I feel happy. For a moment, everything stops. I slow down and wave back. Suddenly my priorities shift, and I remember that life is not about *getting* somewhere; it is about *being* somewhere. Funny, often at the end of my day, my moment with Raymond stands out as one of the highlights of my day.

One day it occurred to me that this young man is making a high and holy contribution to the world. In his own simple way he is bringing light and love to everyone he touches. Meanwhile, many people are plotting and planning how to save the world. He is just doing it. What greater ministry could one undertake?

I began to reflect on the ways that many of us have thought we must bring about world healing. We may write books, form a church, establish a charity or healing center, write letters to the editors of our newspapers, travel to Washington and march for a cause, or fly to a South American rainforest and throw ourselves in front of a bulldozer. Indeed, all these efforts are admirable.

There is, however, one question you must ask before you can determine the real value of your efforts: What is the state of your *spirit* as you do this work? Is your consciousness founded in love, or have you succumbed to fear, judgment, and dissension? Have you become so caught up in the form of what you are doing that you have lost the essence? Have you been seduced into believing that the goal is more about how it looks rather than how you feel? Do you think there is something you need to do first before you can experience joy, or do you remember that the real gift is you, and right where you are is the place to deliver it?

I was invited to address a Hawaii State Department of Education conference for principals, school support workers, and parents. Dr. Herman Aizawa, the state superintendent of schools, opened the gathering by stating, "I believe we need to return to the three Rs."

My God, I thought. Hasn't anything changed? I heard this same speech thirty years ago!

"Yes," Dr. Aizawa went on, "The three Rs: reading, 'riting, and relationship."

Now that got my attention. Could I believe my ears?

"Our self-esteem task force is working to restore true caring in the school system. Our bible is *Chicken Soup for the Soul.* I believe this book should be in every classroom in America, and one story should be read aloud daily."

I almost slid out of my seat. What a miracle to hear this decree from the state superintendent of schools! A consciousness revolution is, indeed, occurring on the planet. The values that you and I hold dear are filtering their way into the institutions and broad-based systems of our world.

We are getting around to discovering that love is the greatest healer. All other modalities pale in the face of true love. A woman in Canada is achieving extraordinary success healing women with eating disorders. She finds emaciated, 50-pound anorexia and bulimia patients in the hospital, takes them to her home, and administers high doses of compassion and caring to them. She cradles them in her arms, rocks them gently, looks into their eyes, and tells them softly: "I love you. You are so beautiful. Please know how much I care about you and want you to live and be happy."

This woman has succeeded in ways that traditional medical or psychological modalities have not. I am not surprised. Eating disorders are a call for love. All diseases are a call for love. In St. Paul's famous letter to the Corinthians, he declares that "love is the greatest of all." Metaphysician Emmet Fox echoed by stating, "It makes no difference how deeply seated may be the trouble, how hopeless the outlook, how muddled the tangle, how great the mistake. A sufficient realization of love will dissolve it all."

We are living in a time when ordinary people are doing extraordinary things. We are taking back our power from idols and institutions and recognizing that real strength abides in delivering our unique gifts. We are declaring, "I claim the strength to heal my life and change my world." We are turning wheelchairs into pulpits. We are establishing our open arms as the healing center. We are recognizing that real education must include relationships. Something good is happening. If you ever feel discouraged, just drive past Raymond's house; he will uncripple your doubts.

For Reflection

1. Do you know anyone who is delivering wisdom or healing in an unpretentious way? Why do you think that person is effective?

2. Do you know people who are engaged in positive social causes but are embroiled in anger or conflict? Do you think they are more effective for their upset, or less?

3. How important is the education of relationship in a school system? If you could write a curriculum for relationship, what would it include?

Whatever Works

*M*y friends' love lives are more interesting than many movies and novels. One night I sat at dinner with two friends and heard two disparate yet compelling accounts: Sam, after living with his girlfriend for three years, had recently moved into his own place. "It feels so good to have my own space again," he reported. "Merrill and I had gotten so bogged down with the issues of our relationship that I was losing touch with who I am. Now I have a sense of myself again, and I feel wonderful!"

Sitting next to Sam, Rob was also glowing—he had just fallen in love. "I never imagined a relationship could be this fulfilling," Rob exclaimed. "Carlie and I are growing deeper every day, and I feel closer to her than any woman I have been with. Each day is a new and wonderful adventure together!"

I basked in the happiness my two friends were exuding. Each of them had found soul satisfaction through antithetical situations—Sam was diving out of relationship, and Rob was diving in. For a moment, my mind tried to judge, "Who is right?" Yet my heart, which values essence more than form, reminded me, "Each is in his perfect place on his path, proven by the experience of joy."

198

The simplest—and most powerful—formula for love is to support the beloved to do what brings him or her joy. We do not have the right or the ability to judge what should make others happy. If we could legislate their actions according to our idea of happiness, then they would have the right to legislate our actions according to their values—and no one would want that. Just ask any teenager!

I have a friend who was in an on-again, off-again relationship. Marcia came to me and told me that she and her boyfriend had finally broken up, and it was a big relief. "That's great!" I told her. "Congratulations!"

A month later she called and told me, "We got back together again, and it feels so right."

"Wonderful!" I responded. "The important thing is that you feel good about it."

Several months later, the story changed again. "We just had to tell the truth that we don't really belong together," Marcia confessed. "Now we both feel free."

"Freedom is where it's at," I concurred.

Then a few weeks later, "We spent the weekend together, just as friends, and we had such a good time that we fell in love all over again."

"Love is where it's at," I affirmed.

And so on. Each time Marcia came to me, I did not try to judge or steer her in a direction of my choosing. I sought to support and empower her in the direction of *her* choosing. She was going to do what she was going to do anyway. She needed a friend more than a judge.

I read about a man who had gone through a deep depression. In *The Active Life,* Parker J. Palmer recounts that many of his friends tried to fix him, except for one. That friend would come to his house every afternoon and simply massage his feet. This man, Palmer notes, was more helpful to him than everyone else who had an agenda for him.

Have you ever dieted? Have you ever read diet books? There are thousands of them, and they all contradict one another. Some say that eating fat causes overweight, and others prove that sugar is the culprit. Others are certain that vegetarianism is the cure for all human ills, while others make a strong case that your blood type determines how much meat you should eat. Others stress fresh fruits and vegetables, while others advocate proper cooking. Others teach that you should drink large quantities of water, yet others say this is dangerous. *Eat Right to Keep Fit* has a very well-integrated system, and so does *The Zone*—and they're different. I know a number of people who practice and advocate drinking one's own urine as a method to cleanse and ward off disease. Holy kidneys, Batman!

Which diet is true? Which is the one for you? Which one really works? The answer is that they *all* work—even the urine one! Everything works for someone, and nothing works for everyone. Go figure. Welcome to Planet Earth, where individual choice supercedes rubber-stamp quick fixes. But that's where the game becomes fun: you just have to figure out what works for you and be true to it. It's that simple and that difficult.

I'll help you make it easier: Follow joy. The only thing more important than what you do is the feeling you experience while doing it. The greatest gift you can give yourself and the world is *enthusiasm*. The word *enthusi-*

asm derives from the Latin *de Teos*, which means "from God." When you are enthusiastic, you are inviting God to show up on Earth in the form of joy.

One evening at a spiritual retreat, just before the participants were to retire, I noticed a woman reading a magazine titled *Emergency: True Stories of Ambulance Calls.* I was shocked. "Josephine," I exclaimed, "how could you read such heavy stuff right before going to sleep?"

"Oh, I enjoy it," she answered. "I work on the rescue squad, and this gives me some good ideas."

Josephine taught me an important lesson about passion, purpose, and judgment. I would not have enjoyed reading that magazine; it was not a match to my interests. But it was a true expression of Josephine's joy, and she was in integrity with it.

The only true measure of success is happiness. If it works for you, it is good. If it doesn't, don't mess around or waste your time. There are as many paths to the mountaintop as there are travelers. Your only job is to stay true to your own path. Let everyone else take the path that belongs to him or her. The truer you are to your path, the more you serve others. You inspire them to find greater life through their own unique choices. Then, as I did during my dinner with my friends, we can honor our differences while celebrating one another's triumphs.

For Reflection

1. Is there something you want to do but have been hesitating because you are wondering if society would think it is right? Do *you* think it is right?

2. Consider someone you know who is very successful materially, but unhappy. Consider another who is not materially successful, but happy. Consider another who is materially successful and happy. What might the lesson be?

3. Can you ever really know what is right for someone else?

Keep the Change

One Easter I was invited to speak at a large church in southern California. The holiday schedule included three ornate services, the first beginning at sunrise. I fondly remember gathering with the minister outside the church at dawn, then marching into the church to the accompaniment of a regal trumpet and a triumphant orchestra. I remember thinking, This must be what heaven is like!

When the second service began, again I entered amidst ruffles and flourishes, and thought, How divine—the celestial orchestra plays on!

By the time the third service came around, I noticed my attitude had changed. As I stood at the same entry point with the same people, watching the same doors open, marching to the same music, I thought, This is getting boring; I sure am glad this is the last time I have to do this. What started out as the Elysian Fields had turned into *Groundhog Day.*

Many of us traditionally picture heaven as a serene realm atop boundless fluffy clouds where white-robed angels float around playing harps all day long—a magnificent image, to be sure. Yet if you were consigned to such a domain, how long do you think you would find this experience heavenly? When you arrived, you would probably

welcome such a scenario—but after a few days it would drive you crazy!

Heaven is not a stagnant place. God is life, and life is about color, variety, creativity, movement, and expansion. The angels-on-clouds scene works when we need rest, but when we are ready to go on to our next adventure, it no longer feels like paradise. As Jesus declared, "In my Father's house there are many mansions." In God's world there are endless stages upon which we play out the odyssey of awakening.

What keeps us growing is not controlling our world so that everything stays just how it has been; what keeps us growing is growth and expansion.

When I began to travel frequently, I noticed that when I was getting ready to leave for an extended trip I would accomplish more goals than I did during the time I had been home. I completed games of phone tag, put away objects I had left around the house, and finished projects that had been hanging out for a while. My desire to be free to enjoy my travels motivated me to handle lots of unfinished business.

When I returned home after traveling, there was another flurry of activity in the direction of new beginnings. My time away from my regular routine gave me space and perspective to see things in a different light, and the people and experiences I encountered on the road stimulated my creativity and desire to expand. Coming home seemed like a natural jumping-off point for new projects.

I recall an important principle I learned in graduate school, where I studied group dynamics. Studies show that when a group of people gets together for a project, the most work gets done at the beginning and ending of a session. (In the U.S. Congress, for example, many bills are introduced at the beginning of a session, there is a lull of accomplishment in the middle, and just before the session closes, many bills are passed or defeated, often at the last tick of the clock.) The more beginnings and endings you create, the more progress you will make. So if you are planning a project that involves creative or work sessions, you will do better to have a larger number of shorter sessions than a smaller number of longer ones.

Trust in change is the bedrock of the entire spiritual path. If you are going through changes that seem beyond your control, quit trying to fight them. If you have faith that God is present, even when it appears otherwise, you are on the track to peace and healing. If you resist change, life will go on anyway, often for the better. In one of my seminars, a woman declared, "Everything I have to let go of, I leave claw marks on." Someone else suggested, "If it walks out of the refrigerator by itself, let it go!"

The story is told about two Zen monks who were walking by the bank of a river on their way to a town several miles downstream. Suddenly a storm overtook them and a flash flood washed the monks into the river. One monk panicked, tried to fight his way back to shore, and drowned. The other monk realized it would do him no good to struggle, and he did his best to relax and move with the energy of the river. Lo and behold, later that day the river deposited him on the shore of the town he was headed toward, in a much shorter time than it would have taken him to walk.

Heaven is not a place you arrive at when you are all

done. It is a state of mind you enjoy as you travel. The journey is as important as the destination. As Emerson eloquently noted, "We may search the world for happiness, but unless we carry it with us, we find it not." Carry love in your heart, and wherever you go, heaven appears.

For Reflection

1. How well do you flow with change? Do you tend to accept it or resist it?

2. Consider any changes occurring in your life now. How might they be part of a perfect plan for your growth and well-being?

3. What is your idea of heaven? Can you visualize heaven not as a static state, but a dynamic flow?

How Long It Took

*I*n the charming French resort town of Nice, an American woman named Joan was shopping in the open-air market one morning when she saw a man who resembled the renowned artist Pablo Picasso. As Joan neared the elderly, energetic fellow, she grew more certain that he was indeed the great painter and one of her idols.

With trepidation, Joan approached the man and asked him, "Excuse me, but aren't you Pablo Picasso?"

"That's right," he answered softly.

Excitement began to exude from every pore of Joan's being. She told him: "I don't mean to disturb you, sir, but I am one of your biggest fans. Is there any way you would be willing to take just a few minutes and do a simple sketch of me? I'd be happy to pay you."

Picasso stepped back a foot or two, studied the woman's features, and then answered with a smile, "Yes, I will."

Joan nearly swooned. Picasso picked up his sketchpad from the foot of a fruit stand, and the two walked to a nearby sidewalk café where they claimed a quiet table off to the side. Picasso opened his pad, reached into his jacket pocket for a small piece of charcoal, and went to work. Fifteen minutes later he turned the pad around and

showed Joan his finished work. It was spectacular—an authentic Picasso, and of her!

Joan took the portrait, embraced it, and thanked the master profusely. Then she opened her purse, took out her checkbook, and asked, "How much will that be?"

"Five thousand dollars," Picasso answered in a matter-of-fact way.

Joan's jaw dropped. "Five thousand dollars? But, sir, the picture took you only fifteen minutes to draw."

"No, madam," he answered quite seriously. "You don't understand. The painting took me eighty years and fifteen minutes to draw."

Everything you have ever done has led you to become who and what you are today. All that you know and do is built on the lessons that paved the way to this rich and precious moment. Every failure and triumph you have charted, every kind heart and charlatan you have encountered, every foray into uncharted territory, and all the information you gleaned have all contributed to your practical wisdom. You stand on the shoulders of all your mistakes, insights, laughter, tears, and years. Indeed, you are taller for it!

In the same way, all your relationships have led you to this point. While you might tend to cringe when you think of your past errors in relationships or resent the partners you are not with anymore, you can appreciate them for the delightful moments you shared and the lessons you learned. I heard about a couple who, during their wedding ceremony, took the time to mention by name their past significant partners and thank them for the gifts they had contributed to their lives. "If it weren't for these relationships," the couple announced, "we would not be the people we are today, standing here together, bringing what we do to each other."

In your career, attribute proper value to the experiences that have seasoned you and your colleagues. When offering your services or negotiating your fee or contract, take into account all the learning that has built the skills you wield. Even if you are inexperienced in a certain field, you can likely transfer the expertise you have gained in another arena. A good salesperson can sell anything; if you know how to sell pool supplies, selling cars is just a matter of learning the details of the industry. Data is far easier to learn than skill. Once you have a skill, you have it for a lifetime.

A famous story tells of a company that needed a boiler repaired. The manager called in a boiler repairman and explained the problem to him. With hardly a thought, the repairman walked to his toolbox and took out a screw driver and a screw. He walked to the boiler, opened a certain small door, replaced the screw, and adjusted it. Immediately the boiler began to work again.

On his way out, the repairman presented the manager with a bill for $100. "One hundred dollars?" exclaimed the manager. "All you did was turn a screw."

"Yes," answered the repairman. "The bill can be broken down as follows: $1 for the screw; $99 for knowing which screw to turn."

Big things are the result of a lot of little things. When you achieve a landmark deal in your business, meet the man or woman of your dreams, or finally feel better after a chronic illness, you are not just lucky and it is not a fluke. Over time and experience you have built the conscious-

ness to generate this shift. The change may seem to be the result of one act or connection, but be assured that everything you have ever done has built up to it.

Former British Prime Minister Margaret Thatcher stated, "One only gets to the top rung on the ladder by steadily climbing up one at a time, and suddenly, all sorts of powers, all sorts of abilities which you thought *never* belonged to you—suddenly become within your own possibility."

We tend to be shortsighted when it comes to our achievements or those of others. Do not be fooled. The Universe operates not by chance, but by scientific principles. Every day, every moment, you are building your consciousness. You are trying many different experiences on for size, and with each one you learn more about who you are, what you want, and how to create your life by choice. Then one day your dream becomes a reality—not in fifteen minutes, but perhaps after many years. Then you truly own it. And it is worth a lot more than $5000.

For Reflection

1. Do you have skills that took a long time to develop? What are they? How did you develop them?

2. Can you acknowledge the blessings of your past relationships? Write down the name(s) of your significant partner(s) and note the gifts you received from the relationship(s).

3. Identify one key turning point in your career, relationship, or health. What chain of events led to that turning point?

Where the Trail Gets Good

One of my favorite hiking trails on Maui leads to a magnificent hidden waterfall far off the beaten path. The footpath to the waterfall begins as an offshoot of a main trail in a county park. One day as I set out on the waterfall trail I noticed that county officials had posted a sign: "End of trail." As I stepped over the sign onto the jungle path, I chuckled to think that what was advertised as the end of the main trail was really the *beginning* of a better trail. If unknowing hikers simply heeded the public sign, they were led to believe their hike was over. If, however, they paid attention to their inner guide, they would discover that the hike was just getting good.

Sometimes it appears that you are at the end of your trail, when you are really at the beginning. If you take your direction from social expectations, you will simply follow the herd and be programmed by what other people think for you. (If you don't use your mind, someone else will.) Many people who formulate social signs are guided by fear and small thinking; there is nothing original or joyful about the well-trod way. If, on the other hand, you follow your inspired inner voice, you will be led to experiences that far surpass any social postings. Buddha said,

"To see what few have seen, you must go where few have gone."

On a cute TV sitcom, *Sabrina the Teenage Witch*, Sabrina accidentally turns her boyfriend into a toad. To rescue him, she must pass a test of true love. Sabrina's initiation brings her to a rope bridge hovering over a fiery chasm, where her beloved awaits on the other side. The bridge catches fire, and if Sabrina is going to get to her young man, she will have to leap—it's now or never. On Sabrina's side of the bridge she sees two signs: "True Love" points over the bridge toward her boyfriend, and "Safe Path" points back from where she came. "Maybe you should just take the safe path!" her boyfriend yells. "No way!" Sabrina answers, "that just leads to the suburbs."

Often our true path is not the apparently safe one—but if we examine the "safe" path, it leads to numbness and limitation. The only real safety lies in being true to yourself. What does your heart tell you is true for you? If you were to live totally authentically, what would you be doing differently? *Realness* will guide you reliably through the many changes happening in and around you. Trust who and what you are, and the Universe will support you.

My friend Donna Lynn sensed that she had played out her executive job, and she yearned for greater career fulfillment. Then her company offered her a position on the night shift. The job was not better but the salary was higher, so she took it. One evening when Donna Lynn visited the ladies' room she noticed that the night cleaning crew was throwing away toilet tissue rolls with a lot of toilet tissue left on them. Donna Lynn considered this practice to be a waste of a valuable resource, so she collected these rolls and took them to a local homeless shelter. Over time she found her involvement with this charity so rewarding that she became a volunteer, then a volunteer coordinator, and eventually went on to a salaried position as director of a citywide volunteer agency. Donna Lynn's work became so successful that she gained national prominence and received an outstanding service award that brought her to Washington, D.C., where she was honored by President and Mrs. Clinton and met several past United States presidents and their spouses—all as a result of a single spontaneous thought about a roll of toilet paper!

I know many people who have experienced abrupt, unexpected, or painful endings in the course of their lives. They have gone through the death or divorce of a spouse, health challenges, job layoffs, and bankruptcies. Many of these people discovered that the experience was the end of something, but it was also the beginning of something. When they stepped into the new lives in which they were thrust, they discovered gifts and blessings that, in many cases, were more rewarding than the stages of the lives they had "lost." So the losses were just stepping-stones to transformation; many of these people reported that their lives really began after their breakups or layoffs.

I met one woman over age sixty who had gotten divorced after forty years of marriage. And did she look radiant! She was fashionably dressed and quite vivacious. She confided to me that during her marriage, all she knew was the role of housewife. "I had no idea how to travel, I was socially inept, and I didn't even know how to write a check!" she told me. "When my husband left, I felt devastated. Then, after I got over my self-pity, I decided I would

jump back into life. And what a jump it has been! I feel happy and in charge of my life!"

If you think you are at the end of your trail, think again—this may be where your adventure really starts to take off!

For Reflection

1. Have you ever experienced an ending that turned out to be a beginning? What happened that made the new beginning meaningful?

2. If you were not concerned about social opinion or approval, what would you be doing differently?

3. How much of your life is motivated by passion? How much is motivated by playing it safe?

How to Make a Fortune

*T*here we sat in the Chinese restaurant, fortune cookies staring us in the face. Will I get a good one? I wondered, as I crumbled the cracker casing and carefully removed the thin strip of paper. When I finally read my fortune, however, it changed me from the inside out. What I saw eventually led to a major course correction in how I approach *everything*. I won't tell you what I read, though—I can't remember—it was boring. All I remember is the wave of disappointment that rippled through my gut; I was hoping for something wonderful, and I got something inane.

I watched my lunch companion open her fortune, and I saw no reaction. "Do you like your fortune?" I asked her.

"Not especially."

How symbolic, I thought. How much of my life have I lived this way? Someone tells me who I am, who I should be, how I should live, and what is going to happen to me— and I just go along with the notion because that is what is set before me. How many millions of people live dull, meaningless "lives of quiet desperation," just going on in the same way because all they know about how they should live is what others have told them?

Suddenly it dawned on me: this didn't have to be the end of the story.

"Waitress!" I called out.

"Yes, sir?"

"We really don't care for the fortunes we've received," I told her authoritatively. "Would you please bring us some more?"

She smiled and answered, "Sure."

A minute later our waitress returned with *a whole bowl* of fortune cookies. The Universe not only answered my request, but also *magnified* it! The waitress gingerly set the bowl on the table and announced, "Here—take your pick." So we did. We went through the bowl, unraveling fortunes until we each found one we wanted.

Here we have a wonderful metaphor for all of life: *You can take what you are given, or you can make what you want.* If you like what you have, then bless it and enjoy it; if not, you can call the waitress and ask for a new selection.

Today would be a good day to make your own fortune. Ask yourself, "What would I love to happen?" Then follow the voice that brings you the greatest aliveness, and you are on your way to living your highest potential.

Your future is not set in stone; it is molded with love. You create and re-create your future in every moment, with every choice you make. A psychic, seer, or prophet may be able to look down the road and see likely outcomes of actions and energies currently in motion. (A Zen aphorism suggests, "If you do not change direction, you will end up where you are headed.") But at any moment a human being—a *spiritual* being—can craft a new decision and alter the course of events. Because God has imbued us with the power to create, we are always free to create a new destiny.

There is no force outside you that determines what happens to you. *You* are the force that engineers your destiny. Walt Whitman declared: "I do not seek good fortune. I *am* good fortune." The power or help you have been seeking in the outer world already lives inside you, *as* you. Luck is not a capricious gift that whimsically falls into our laps; it is a stream we attract with our thoughts, feelings, attitudes, words, and actions. I saw a *Ziggy* cartoon in which our hero explains, "I have a rabbit's foot, a four-leaf clover, and a lucky charm—only problem is, none of them become effective until I do."

If you are waiting for your ship to come in, why not build your own boat? If you are waiting for a particular person to come along and make your life wonderful, that person is you. The more you love yourself, the greater your power to draw unto you loving companions. At this very moment you have everything you need to set into motion a chain of events that will change your life forever.

When considering fortunes projected onto you by others, remember the immortal words of movie mogul Samuel Goldwyn: "Never make forecasts, especially about the future."

For Reflection

1. What do you believe is your role in creating your future?

2. Are you still living out any programs or expectations set for you by your parents, teachers, religion, family, or friends? If you were not subject to those expectations, what would you be doing differently?

3. Think of someone you admire who has taken charge of his or her life and lifted it to a new level. How did that person do it?

The Ending Doesn't Matter

*B*illy Elliot is the brilliant cinematic saga of an eleven-year-old British boy who wants to become a classical ballet dancer. Billy's plight is especially challenging because he lives in a very macho home and town where men are expected to be manly men, and his family wants him to be a boxer. Billy's father and older brother, both manly men, find his dance aspirations utterly abhorrent, for they equate them with being a sissy or homosexual. As a result, they do everything they can to squash Billy's vision and turn him into a "real" boy.

But Billy's ambitions are stronger than his family's objections, and he pursues his dream in spite of their opposition. Eventually Billy gains a shot at being accepted to a prestigious dance academy, which would offer him a hope of turning his dream into a real career. At first, Billy's family members dismiss the notion as utterly preposterous, but over time they realize that he is sincere, and they grow to support him in his quest. In the process, his father and brother come to heal their deep-seated animosity toward each other. Ultimately, after a great deal of conflict and torment, the family is united in its efforts to get Billy into the dance program.

The drama leads to a crucial scene in which Billy receives the long-awaited letter from the dance academy, informing him as to whether or not he has been accepted. The movie's director does a remarkable job building and milking the tension around opening the letter; I was on the edge of my seat, nearly biting my fingernails waiting to find out if Billy had gotten in.

So as not to spoil the movie for you, I will not tell you the ending. But I will tell you what I felt as I waited to learn what the letter said: *it didn't matter.* Whether or not Billy was accepted to the dance school was less important than what had happened to him and his family in the process of his application. As he held fast to his ideals in the face of massive resistance, he developed immense soul strength. At the same time, his family members experienced the healing of a lifetime as they learned to support him and resolve the deep resentments they had etched over many years. The invaluable life lessons they all learned far outshined whether or not he was accepted to the academy. No matter what the letter said, they all triumphed, and a happy ending was assured.

It is easy to be seduced by the idea that how things turn out is more important than what happens in the process. Manifestations, as desirable as they are, are by-products of the soul qualities we develop in our quest for the goal. The real question is not, "How did it turn out?" The real question is, "What happened to your spirit as you journeyed?"

I studied with a healer who told me that two of his most profound healings occurred with people who passed on soon afterward. "How could that be?" I asked him. He explained: "These people experienced a spiritual healing;

their souls came to peace before they passed. Yes, it is important to try to heal the body, but it is more important to heal the spirit."

In my seminars, I often work with people who are struggling with having been divorced. Many talk about the "failure" of their marriages. I asked one fellow, "How long were you married?"

"Twenty years," he answered.

"And were you happy most of that time?" I asked.

"Yes, we had a good marriage for many of those years. It was just during the last few years that our relationship unraveled."

"Then why discount the gifts of those good years just because it didn't last forever?" I asked him.

Just because a marriage (or anything) ends, doesn't mean it failed. Ideally, of course, we would like a marriage to last for a lifetime. But when it doesn't, we dishonor the relationship by casting an aura of failure over all of it. If you loved, learned, and grew during the time you were together, there was real success. The relationship is a failure only if you learned nothing and you go on to repeat the same mistakes. And even if you do, all your experience is contributing to ultimate learning, so it is all part of your soul's growth.

I find it interesting that, in contrast to other life adventures, we make separate rules of judgment about marriage and relationships. If you stay in a job or a home or a friendship for ten or twenty years, and then you resign, move, or grow apart, you don't say, "My job (or home or friendship) failed." You acknowledge that the experience served an important purpose during the time you were in it. Then, when it no longer is a source of life and joy, you acknowledge that you have grown, changed, or moved on; you appreciate its gifts and release it with love. When it comes to marriage, however, we are taught that we have failed unless we stay together for a lifetime. This seems rather harsh to me.

Let's begin to celebrate our lives as an adventure in dynamic unfoldment. Of course we want it to turn out in the way we would like, but when it doesn't, there are many other gifts available, gifts often far more meaningful than grabbing the brass ring. The real brass ring is the joy of the journey. Just ask Billy.

For Reflection

1. Is there a situation in your life in which you feel like a failure? Is there a way you can regard the situation as a success, even though it didn't turn out as you had hoped?

2. What was the most challenging experience of your life? What soul muscles did you build in dealing with it?

3. Are you more goal-oriented or process-oriented? What are the strong points and the pitfalls of each path?

About the Author

Alan Cohen is the author of sixteen popular inspirational books including the best-selling *The Dragon Doesn't Live Here Anymore* and the award-winning *A Deep Breath of Life.* Alan is a contributing writer for the *New York Times* #1 best-selling series *Chicken Soup for the Soul.* His books have been translated into twelve foreign languages.

Each month Alan's column, *From the Heart,* is published in sixty magazines internationally. His interviews and articles have been celebrated in *Unity Magazine, Science of Mind, New Woman, First for Women, Personal Transformation, New Realities, Human Potential,* and *Visions* magazines.

A frequent guest on radio and television, Alan has appeared on CNBC's *America's Talking* as well as many other shows throughout the nation. His presentations are regularly broadcast via satellite on the Wisdom Channel, and he is a faculty member at Omega Institute in New York. Alan has served as a consultant to organizations throughout the United States, Europe, Australia, the former Soviet Union, Scandinavia, and Greece. He also guides groups on excursions to sacred sites such as Machu Picchu, Bali, and Egypt.

Alan resides in Maui, Hawaii, where he conducts retreats in visionary living.

For information on Alan Cohen's books, tapes, Hawaii

About the Author

retreats, journeys to sacred sites, online prosperity course, and seminars in your area:

Visit: www.spiritfirst.com
E-mail: admin@alancohen.com
Phone: 800-568-3079
Fax: 808-572-1023, or
Write to: Alan Cohen Programs and Publications
P.O. Box 835
Haiku, HI 96708

Printed in the U.S.A.   189-0523-4M-8-02